HENRY HANLEY

Unveiling

GAME DESIGN

FROM CONCEPTS TO CREATIONS

The Allure of Video Games and the Creative Processes Behind Them

In today's modern culture, video games have seamlessly woven themselves into the fabric of society, captivating a vast global audience and reaping tremendous financial success. They possess an unparalleled capacity to whisk us away to wondrous realms, stimulating our imagination and immersing us in experiences that surpass the boundaries of any other medium. Yet, behind the curtain, a dedicated and gifted team toils tirelessly to breathe life into these virtual landscapes. At the core of their creative efforts lies the artistry and craftsmanship of game design.

The allure of video games stems from their ability to offer interactive storytelling, engaging gameplay mechanics, and visually stunning experiences. As players, we become active participants in these virtual worlds, shaping the narrative, overcoming challenges, and making consequential decisions. The emotional impact games can have on us is profound, evoking excitement, joy, fear, and even empathy. They can transport us to distant galaxies, medieval kingdoms, post-apocalyptic wastelands, or create entirely unique and imaginative settings that defy reality.

Behind every captivating game lies a creative process that merges artistic vision, technical expertise, and player-centric design principles. The game design process serves as the foundation upon which the entire development cycle is built. It is a delicate dance between artistry and technology, requiring a deep understanding of player psychology, market trends, and the technical limitations of the medium.

Game designers play a pivotal role in this process, serving as the architects who conceive and shape the virtual worlds players will explore. They are the masterminds who create game mechanics, design compelling narratives, craft immersive environments, and weave together audiovisual elements to create memorable experiences. They possess a unique blend of creativity, analytical thinking, and problem-solving skills.

The creative process behind game design is a multifaceted journey that starts with the initial spark of an idea. From there, designers delve into research and analysis, studying player preferences, market trends, and the potential for innovation. They develop a concept that captures the essence of their vision, working on a game design document (GDD) that outlines the gameplay mechanics, narrative elements, visual style, and other crucial aspects.

Prototyping and iteration play a vital role in the game design process. Designers create early versions of the game, testing and refining gameplay mechanics, level design, and overall player experience. This iterative process allows them to fine-tune their ideas and address any issues or imbalances that arise. Collaboration with other team members, such as artists, programmers, and sound designers, is crucial during this stage, as they collectively bring the game to life.

The production phase involves building the game's framework, implementing assets, and refining the gameplay based on feedback and testing. It requires a delicate balance between creativity and project management, ensuring that the vision of the game is realized within the constraints of time and resources. The art and audio design further enhance the immersive experience, with captivating visuals, stunning animations, and an enchanting soundtrack that evokes the desired emotions.

However, the creative process doesn't end with the game's launch. Game designers must navigate the complexities of the post-production phase, including marketing, distribution, and ongoing support. They analyze player feedback, address bugs and issues, and may even release updates and expansions to keep the game fresh and engaging.

The allure of video games lies not only in the end product but also in the creative process itself. It is a journey that allows designers to blend their passions for art, technology, and storytelling. It pushes the boundaries of innovation, embracing new technologies, and exploring emerging trends like virtual reality, augmented reality, and artificial intelligence.

In this book, we will delve into the world of professional game design, unravelling the intricate steps, methodologies, and challenges involved in creating a game from scratch. We will explore the diverse skill set required, including the ability to think critically, problem-solve, communicate effectively, and collaborate with multidisciplinary teams. We will uncover the secrets behind concept development, pre-production planning, prototyping, production, art and audio design, quality assurance, and post-production support.

Throughout this journey, we will also address the business side of game design, delving into the industry landscape, monetization models, intellectual property considerations, and strategies for building a sustainable career in the field. We will explore the challenges faced by game designers, such as managing scope, time constraints, and player expectations, while also discussing the future trends and innovations that are shaping the industry.

This book aims to provide aspiring game designers, as well as enthusiasts and curious individuals, with an in-depth understanding of the creative process that goes into making a game in the professional world. Whether you dream of creating your own indie game, working in a renowned game studio, or simply want to appreciate the craft behind your favourite games, the insights and knowledge shared in this book will serve as a valuable resource.

By the end of this journey, you will have gained a comprehensive overview of game design, from the initial concept to the final product. You will have a deeper understanding of the iterative nature of the creative process, the importance of player-centric design, and the collaborative efforts required to bring a game to life. You will also be equipped with practical insights, tips, and industry knowledge that will help you navigate the intricate world of game design.

Embark on this adventure as we peel back the curtain and unveil the magic that lies behind the allure of video games. Together, let us explore the creative process that captivates and inspires millions, and uncover the artistry, innovation, and dedication that make video games an extraordinary medium of expression and entertainment.

Chapter 1 - Understanding Game Design

Game design can be defined as the creative and iterative process of conceptualizing, structuring, and shaping the rules, mechanics, aesthetics, and overall experience of a game. It involves the deliberate and thoughtful design decisions made by game designers to create engaging, immersive, and interactive experiences for players. Game design encompasses various elements, such as gameplay mechanics, level design, narrative, aesthetics, and player psychology, all working together to create a cohesive and enjoyable gaming experience.

Game design is a multidisciplinary field that draws from art, technology, psychology, storytelling, and interaction design, among others, to craft games that entertain, challenge, and captivate players. It is a dynamic and iterative process that involves prototyping, playtesting, and refining ideas to create compelling gameplay and foster player engagement. Ultimately, game design is about creating experiences that entertain, inspire, and leave a lasting impact on players.

Game Mechanics

Game mechanics refer to the rules, systems, and interactions that govern gameplay in a video game. They are the building blocks that define how players interact with the game world and each other. Game mechanics encompass a wide range of elements, including movement, combat, puzzles, resource management, character abilities, and progression systems.

In relation to game design, mechanics are essential as they provide the structure and framework for player actions and decisions. They shape the core gameplay experience, influencing the challenges players face, the strategies they employ, and the goals they strive to achieve. Well-designed game mechanics are crucial for creating engaging and balanced gameplay that keeps players motivated and invested.

Game designers carefully design and balance mechanics to ensure that they provide meaningful choices and interactions for players. They consider factors such as difficulty, skill progression, pacing, and player agency when crafting mechanics. By designing mechanics that are intuitive, enjoyable, and aligned with the game's overall vision, designers can create a compelling gameplay experience that resonates with players.

Moreover, game mechanics often work in harmony with other elements of game design, such as level design, narrative, and aesthetics. They can enhance storytelling by providing gameplay elements that reinforce the narrative themes or create immersive and atmospheric experiences. Mechanics can also be used to create social interactions, cooperative or competitive gameplay, and emergent gameplay possibilities, adding depth and replayability to a game.

Overall, game mechanics are a fundamental aspect of game design, serving as the rules and systems that shape player interactions and gameplay experiences. They contribute to the overall enjoyment, challenge, and depth of a game, making them a vital consideration for game designers.

Level Design

Level design, in the context of game design, refers to the creation and arrangement of game environments, challenges, and experiences within a video game. It involves designing the individual levels, stages, or areas that players navigate through during gameplay. Level design encompasses the layout, structure, pacing, and interactive elements within each level, all with the aim of providing engaging and enjoyable gameplay experiences.

Level design plays a crucial role in shaping the player's journey and overall game experience. It involves carefully crafting the physical spaces, obstacles, puzzles, enemies, and rewards that players encounter as they progress through the game. Level designers consider factors such as difficulty progression, player exploration, and the balance between challenge and reward to create compelling and balanced gameplay.

The goals of level design may vary depending on the genre and style of the game. In a platformer, level design focuses on platform placement, jump distances, and timing challenges. In a first-person shooter, level design revolves around creating strategic paths, cover opportunities, and varied combat encounters. In an open-world game, level design includes creating a seamless and immersive world with diverse locations and activities for players to explore.

Collaboration lies at the core of level design, as level designers closely collaborate with a multidisciplinary team, including artists, programmers, and game designers, to ensure a seamless integration of levels within the game's overarching vision and gameplay mechanics. By taking into account the aesthetics, audio design, and narrative elements, level designers craft immersive and cohesive experiences that harmonize with the gameplay. Through this collaborative effort, the team strives to create levels that not only challenge and engage players but also enhance the overall atmosphere and storytelling, elevating the game to new heights of immersion and enjoyment.

Effective level design engages players, encourages exploration, and provides a sense of progression and achievement. It aims to strike a balance between challenge and player skill, offering both moments of difficulty and opportunities for success. Well-designed levels can evoke emotions, tell stories, and create memorable experiences for players, enhancing the overall quality and enjoyment of a video game.

Narrative

Narrative in game design refers to the storytelling elements and structure within a video game. It encompasses the plot, characters, dialogue, world-building, and overall storytelling techniques employed to create a cohesive and immersive narrative experience for players.

In game design, narrative serves as a means to engage players on an emotional and intellectual level, providing context, purpose, and motivation for their actions within the game world. It can take various forms, ranging from linear, scripted narratives to non-linear, player-driven storytelling experiences.

The narrative elements in a game can include:

Plot: The overarching story arc or sequence of events that unfold throughout the game. It typically involves conflict, challenges, and character development.

Characters: The individuals, both playable and non-playable, who populate the game world. They have their own backgrounds, motivations, and roles within the narrative.

Dialogue: The spoken or written exchanges between characters, providing context, conveying information, and progressing the story.

World-building: The creation of a rich and immersive game world with its own history, lore, geography, and culture. World-building enhances the narrative by providing a sense of depth and realism.

Quests and Missions: Specific objectives or tasks that players undertake to advance the narrative. They may involve solving puzzles, defeating enemies, or making impactful choices that shape the story.

Game designers use various techniques to integrate narrative elements into gameplay, such as cutscenes, in-game dialogue, environmental storytelling, and interactive storytelling mechanics. They strive to create a harmonious balance between gameplay and storytelling, ensuring that the narrative elements enhance the player's engagement and emotional investment in the game.

Narrative in game design has the potential to evoke emotions, immerse players in a fictional world, convey themes and messages, and provide a sense of progression and purpose. Well-crafted narratives can deepen the player's connection to the game, making their experience more meaningful and memorable.

Aesthetics

Aesthetics, in the context of game design, refers to the visual and auditory elements that contribute to the overall look, feel, and atmosphere of a video game. It encompasses the art direction, graphics, sound design, music, and user interface design, all of which work together to create a cohesive and immersive experience for players.

In game design, aesthetics play a vital role in captivating players, setting the mood, and enhancing the overall experience. They help establish the game's unique identity, evoke emotions, and create a sense of immersion in the game world. Aesthetics can vary widely depending on the artistic style and thematic choices of the game, ranging from realistic and detailed visuals to stylized and abstract designs.

Here are some key aspects of aesthetics in game design:

Art Direction: The overall visual style and direction of the game, including the choice of color palettes, art styles, and graphical fidelity. Art direction sets the tone and establishes the visual identity of the game.

Graphics: The visual representation of the game world, characters, objects, and environments. Graphics encompass the quality of textures, lighting effects, particle systems, and other visual elements that contribute to the game's visual appeal.

Sound Design: The creation and implementation of audio elements in the game. Sound design includes the use of ambient sounds, background music, character voices, and sound effects to enhance the atmosphere and create an immersive auditory experience.

Music: The composition and integration of music into the game. Music sets the mood, reinforces the narrative, and heightens emotional moments. It can range from ambient soundscapes to dynamic and interactive musical scores.

User Interface Design: The visual design and layout of the game's user interface, including menus, HUD (Heads-Up Display), icons, and interactive elements. User interface design aims to provide clarity, ease of use, and aesthetic coherence, ensuring a smooth and enjoyable player experience.

Aesthetics in game design go beyond visual and auditory elements; they also encompass the emotional impact and the overall experience created for players. Well-crafted aesthetics can immerse players in the game world, enhance the narrative, evoke emotions, and leave a lasting impression. By carefully considering and implementing aesthetics, game designers can create visually stunning and captivating experiences that resonate with players.

Player Psychology

Player psychology, in the context of game design, refers to the understanding and consideration of the cognitive, emotional, and behavioural aspects of players when designing a video game. It involves analyzing how players think, feel, and behave in response to game mechanics, challenges, rewards, and overall gameplay experiences.

By incorporating principles of player psychology into game design, developers can create more engaging, immersive, and enjoyable experiences for players.

Here are some key aspects of player psychology in game design:

Motivation: Understanding what motivates players to engage with a game and continue playing. This can include intrinsic motivators such as a sense of accomplishment, curiosity, and mastery, as well as extrinsic motivators such as rewards, achievements, and social recognition.

Flow: Creating gameplay experiences that strike a balance between challenge and skill, leading to a state of "flow" where players are fully immersed and engaged in the game. Flow occurs when the difficulty of the game matches the player's skill level, providing a sense of flow and optimal challenge.

Player Types: Recognizing that players have different preferences, play styles, and motivations. Game designers may consider player typologies, such as Bartle's Player Types (achievers, explorers, socializers, and killers), to tailor gameplay experiences to different player preferences.

Emotions: Recognizing the emotional impact games can have on players and designing experiences that evoke specific emotions. Games can elicit a wide range of emotions, including excitement, joy, fear, sadness, and surprise, which can enhance player engagement and attachment to the game.

Cognitive Load: Considering the cognitive load placed on players, including information processing, decision-making, and memory. Game designers aim to create experiences that are cognitively challenging but not overwhelming, ensuring that players can effectively process information and make meaningful choices.

Player Feedback: Providing clear and meaningful feedback to players about their actions, progress, and achievements. Feedback can help players understand the consequences of their decisions, gauge their performance, and adjust their strategies accordingly.

By taking into account player psychology, game designers can create experiences that resonate with players, keep them engaged, and provide a sense of satisfaction and enjoyment. Through an understanding of how players think, feel, and behave, designers can tailor their games to meet the needs and preferences of their target audience, ultimately creating more compelling and immersive gameplay experiences.

Exploring the roles and responsibilities of a game designer

The role of a game designer encompasses a wide range of responsibilities, as they are responsible for conceptualizing, designing, and overseeing the development of video games.

Here are some key roles and responsibilities of a game

designer:

Game Conceptualization: Game designers are involved in the initial stages of game development, where they generate ideas and concepts for new games. They develop the overall vision, theme, and mechanics that will shape the gameplay experience.

Game Mechanics Design: Game designers are responsible for designing the core mechanics and rules that govern gameplay. This includes defining player actions, interactions, progression systems, and balancing the game's difficulty and challenge.

Level and Environment Design: Game designers create and design the levels, environments, and spaces within the game. They determine the layout, placement of objects, obstacles, and enemy encounters to ensure engaging and balanced gameplay experiences.

Narrative Design: In collaboration with writers and narrative designers, game designers contribute to the creation of the game's story, characters, and overall narrative structure. They help integrate the narrative elements into the gameplay to create a cohesive and immersive experience.

Prototyping and Iteration: Game designers create early prototypes of the game to test and refine gameplay mechanics, level designs, and overall player experience. They iterate on their designs based on playtesting feedback, making adjustments to improve the game's quality and playability.

Collaboration and Communication: In the realm of game design, collaboration and communication form the cornerstone of success. Game designers forge close partnerships with various members of the development team, including artists, programmers, sound designers, and producers. This collaboration is essential to ensure that the game's design harmonizes with the artistic direction, technical feasibility, and overarching project objectives.

Effective communication skills play a pivotal role in conveying design ideas, providing constructive feedback, and fostering a unified and cohesive development process. Through open and clear lines of communication, game designers facilitate a collaborative environment that nurtures creativity and propels the project towards its desired vision.

Documentation and Documentation: Game designers create design documents and documentation that outline the game's design principles, mechanics, level layouts, and other crucial details. These documents serve as a reference for the development team and help maintain a clear vision throughout the production process.

Playtesting and Balancing: Game designers conduct playtesting sessions to gather feedback from players and identify areas that require improvement. They analyze player behaviour, address issues, and make adjustments to ensure a balanced and enjoyable gameplay experience.

Game Evaluation and Analysis: Game designers evaluate the success of their designs by analyzing player feedback, reviews, and sales data. They assess the impact of their design choices, identify areas of improvement, and apply lessons learned to future projects.

It's important to note that the specific roles and responsibilities of a game designer may vary depending on the size of the development team, the scope of the project, and the studio's organizational structure. However, game designers are generally involved in multiple aspects of game development, combining creativity, analytical thinking, and a deep understanding of player experience to shape compelling and immersive games.

Key skills and qualities required for success

To excel as a game designer, several key skills and qualities are essential.

These include:

Creativity: Game designers must possess a strong creative mindset, as they are responsible for generating innovative ideas, unique concepts, and engaging gameplay experiences. They should be able to think outside the box and come up with imaginative solutions to design challenges.

Critical Thinking: Game designers need strong analytical and critical thinking skills to evaluate and refine their designs. They must be able to identify potential issues, anticipate player experiences, and make informed decisions to enhance gameplay mechanics, level design, and overall player engagement.

Problem-Solving: Game designers encounter various problems throughout the development process, and the ability to solve them efficiently is crucial. They must possess strong problem-solving skills to overcome technical limitations, balance gameplay elements, and address player feedback effectively.

Communication: Effective communication is vital for game designers to convey their design ideas, collaborate with team members, and provide constructive feedback. They should be able to articulate their vision clearly, actively listen to others, and adapt their communication style to various stakeholders.

Collaboration: Game design is a collaborative process, and designers must work closely with artists, programmers, writers, and other team members. Strong collaboration skills, including teamwork, compromise, and respect for others' expertise, are essential to create a cohesive and successful game.

Understanding of Player Experience: A deep understanding of player psychology and player experience is crucial for game designers. They should be able to empathize with players, anticipate their needs and preferences, and design gameplay elements that provide a rewarding and enjoyable experience.

Adaptability: Flexibility is crucial in the game development realm, as it undergoes perpetual transformations. Game designers must possess adaptability, embracing emerging technologies, design trends, and industry breakthroughs in their creations. Remaining up-to-date and skillful in an ever-changing field demands a willingness to learn and adapt.

Attention to Detail: Game designers must have a keen eye for detail to ensure that their designs are polished and coherent. They need to pay attention to elements such as level layout, user interface design, and game mechanics to create a seamless and immersive player experience.

Passion for Games: Ultimately, a genuine passion for games is a key driver for success as a game designer. A love for playing and understanding various genres and styles of games helps designers develop a deep appreciation for what makes a game engaging, enjoyable, and memorable.

Why is creativity skills essential for a games designer?

Creativity is essential for a game designer because it serves as the foundation for innovation and originality in game development.

Here are some reasons why creativity skills are crucial for a game designer:

Unique Game Concepts: Creativity allows game designers to generate fresh and unique ideas for game concepts. By thinking outside the box, they can create innovative gameplay mechanics, compelling narratives, and immersive worlds that set their games apart from others in the market.

Engaging Gameplay Experiences: Creative game design leads to captivating and engaging gameplay experiences. Designers who think creatively can craft gameplay mechanics that are intuitive, interactive, and enjoyable. They can come up with novel ways to challenge players, introduce surprises, and evoke emotions, keeping players engaged and invested in the game.

Problem Solving: Creativity plays a vital role in problem-solving during game development. Designers often encounter obstacles or limitations, such as technical constraints or gameplay imbalances. Creative thinking allows them to find innovative solutions, workarounds, and alternative approaches to overcome these challenges and create better player experiences.

Player-Centric Design: Creative game designers put players at the center of their design process. By thinking creatively, they can empathize with players, understand their desires and preferences, and design games that cater to their needs. This player-centric approach helps create meaningful and enjoyable experiences that resonate with the target audience.

Innovation and Industry Advancement: Creativity is a driving force behind innovation and pushing the boundaries of game design. Game designers who embrace creativity contribute to the evolution of the industry by introducing new concepts, mechanics, and approaches. They inspire other designers and push the medium forward.

Artistic Expression: Games are an artistic medium, and creativity allows designers to express themselves artistically. They can use their creativity to design visually stunning environments, develop unique art styles, compose original soundtracks, and craft narratives that evoke emotions and create memorable experiences.

Competitive Advantage: In a highly competitive industry, creativity gives game designers a competitive edge. Unique and innovative games stand out in the market and attract attention from players and industry professionals. Creative designs can lead to critical acclaim, awards, and commercial success.

Creativity is essential for game designers because it enables them to generate unique ideas, craft engaging gameplay experiences, solve problems, design with the player in mind, drive industry innovation, express artistic vision, and gain a competitive advantage. It is the fuel that propels game design forward and allows designers to create extraordinary and unforgettable gaming experiences.

Why is critical thinking skills essential for a games designer?

Critical thinking skills are essential for a game designer because they enable them to analyze, evaluate, and make informed decisions throughout the game development process.

Here are some reasons why critical thinking skills are crucial for a game designer:

Problem Identification and Solving: Game designers encounter various challenges and obstacles during development, ranging from technical limitations to gameplay issues. Critical thinking skills help designers identify and define problems, analyze their root causes, and develop effective strategies to address them. They can assess the impact of design choices, evaluate potential solutions, and make informed decisions to create better gameplay experiences.

Gameplay Balancing: Balancing gameplay elements, such as difficulty, progression, and player rewards, is a crucial aspect of game design. Critical thinking allows designers to analyze player behaviour and feedback, assess the impact of changes, and fine-tune the game's mechanics to create a balanced and enjoyable experience. They can make adjustments to ensure that the game offers an appropriate level of challenge and rewards players appropriately.

Evaluation of Design Choices: Critical thinking enables game designers to evaluate the strengths and weaknesses of their design choices objectively. They can assess the impact of mechanics, level design, narrative elements, and other components on the overall player experience. By critically analyzing their designs, designers can identify areas for improvement, refine their ideas, and make informed decisions to enhance the quality of the game.

Player-Centric Design: Critical thinking allows designers to put themselves in the players' shoes and evaluate the game from their perspective. They can anticipate player needs, preferences, and expectations, considering factors such as usability, accessibility, and player enjoyment. By critically evaluating the player experience, designers can make design decisions that prioritize the player and create engaging and satisfying gameplay moments.

Iterative Design Process: Game development often involves an iterative process of prototyping, testing, and refining. Critical thinking skills help designers analyze player feedback, evaluate the success of design iterations, and make informed decisions on how to improve the game. They can identify areas that require adjustment, fine-tune mechanics, and iterate on their designs to create a polished and immersive experience.

Analysing Trends and Market Demands: Critical thinking allows game designers to assess industry trends, player preferences, and market demands. They can analyze market research, player data, and feedback from the gaming community to make informed design decisions that align with current trends and cater to the target audience's needs and desires.

Risk Assessment and Mitigation: Critical thinking enables game designers to assess potential risks and anticipate challenges that may arise during development. They can identify potential pitfalls, evaluate the feasibility of design choices, and develop contingency plans to mitigate risks. This helps ensure smoother development processes and minimizes setbacks.

Critical thinking skills are crucial for game designers as they facilitate problem-solving, gameplay balancing, objective evaluation of design choices, player-centric design, iterative development, analysis of market trends, and risk assessment. By applying critical thinking, game designers can make informed decisions, create high-quality games, and deliver exceptional gameplay experiences to players.

Why are problem solving skills essential for a games designer?

Problem-solving skills are essential for a game designer because they enable them to overcome challenges, find innovative solutions, and ensure the smooth progression of game development.

Here are some reasons why problem-solving skills are crucial for a game designer:

Overcoming Technical Limitations: Game development often involves working with technology and tools that may have limitations or constraints. Problem-solving skills allow designers to find creative workarounds and solutions to overcome technical hurdles. They can adapt and optimize their designs to fit within technical constraints without compromising the gameplay experience.

Balancing Gameplay Elements: Game designers need to

strike a balance between various gameplay elements such as difficulty, progression, and player rewards. Problem-solving skills help designers identify gameplay imbalances, analyze player feedback, and find solutions to create a balanced and satisfying experience. They can tweak mechanics, adjust level design, and fine-tune gameplay progression to address any issues that arise.

Iterative Design Process: Game development often involves an iterative process of prototyping, testing, and refining. Problem-solving skills help designers analyze feedback, identify design flaws, and iterate on their designs. They can identify problems early on, develop alternative solutions, and implement improvements to enhance the overall game experience.

Adapting to Player Feedback: Listening to player feedback is crucial for creating a successful game. Problem-solving skills allow designers to interpret player feedback, identify patterns and trends, and address concerns or issues raised by players. They can analyze the feedback objectively, identify underlying problems, and find creative solutions that align with the players' needs and expectations.

Designing Engaging Mechanics: Creating compelling and engaging gameplay mechanics requires problem-solving skills. Designers need to analyze player behavior, anticipate player needs and desires, and design mechanics that provide meaningful and satisfying interactions. They must solve the challenge of creating mechanics that are intuitive, enjoyable, and align with the game's overall vision.

Addressing Design Challenges: Game design involves various challenges, such as creating immersive worlds, designing complex puzzles, or integrating narrative elements seamlessly. Problem-solving skills allow designers to tackle these challenges head-on, break them down into manageable components, and find effective solutions. They can devise creative solutions to design problems, think outside the box, and push the boundaries of what is possible in game design.

Navigating Development Constraints: Game development often operates within constraints such as time, budget, and resource limitations. Problem-solving skills help designers make efficient use of available resources, prioritize tasks, and navigate these constraints effectively. They can find ways to optimize development processes, streamline workflows, and deliver high-quality games within the given constraints.

Problem-solving skills are crucial for game designers as they enable them to overcome technical limitations, balance gameplay elements, navigate the iterative design process, adapt to player feedback, design engaging mechanics, address design challenges, and navigate development constraints. By applying problem-solving skills, game designers can create exceptional games that provide enjoyable experiences for players.

Why is communication skills essential for a games designer?

Strong communication skills are a cornerstone of success for game designers, enabling them to forge collaborative partnerships, express their design concepts, and uphold a cohesive development process.

The significance of effective communication in game design cannot be overstated, as it empowers designers in the following ways:

Collaboration with Team Members: Game designers work closely with various team members, including artists, programmers, sound designers, and producers. Effective communication skills enable designers to collaborate seamlessly with these team members. They can articulate their design vision, provide clear instructions, and actively listen to others' perspectives, fostering a collaborative and productive work environment.

Conveying Design Ideas: Game designers need to effectively communicate their design ideas to team members and stakeholders. Whether through written documentation, verbal explanations, or visual presentations, strong communication skills allow designers to articulate their creative vision, ensuring that others understand and share their vision for the game. Clear communication helps align everyone's efforts towards a unified design goal.

Providing and Receiving Feedback: Communication skills are essential for giving and receiving feedback during the design process. Designers must provide constructive feedback to team members, such as artists or programmers, to ensure that the game's design aligns with their vision. Additionally, designers need to be open to receiving feedback from others and incorporating valuable insights into their designs. Effective communication facilitates a constructive feedback loop that improves the overall quality of the game.

Bridging Artistic and Technical Perspectives: Game designers often act as a bridge between artistic and technical team members. They need to effectively communicate between these two domains, translating artistic concepts and design requirements into technical specifications that can be implemented by programmers and artists. Strong communication skills help bridge the gap and foster a shared understanding between different disciplines.

Presenting Ideas to Stakeholders: Game designers often need to present their design ideas to stakeholders, such as publishers, executives, or investors. Effective communication skills enable designers to convey the unique selling points of their game, showcase its potential, and garner support for their vision. They can communicate the game's marketability, target audience, and gameplay innovations with clarity and persuasion.

Resolving Conflicts and Negotiation: Game development

can involve conflicts or differences of opinion among team members. Effective communication skills allow designers to navigate conflicts, negotiate compromises, and find mutually beneficial solutions. They can engage in constructive discussions, listen to different viewpoints, and work towards consensus, ensuring that the design process remains collaborative and productive.

Documenting Design Concepts: Communication skills are crucial for documenting design concepts, game mechanics, and design guidelines. Clear and concise documentation helps convey design intentions, ensuring that team members have a comprehensive understanding of the game's design. Well-written design documents facilitate efficient implementation and reduce the chances of misinterpretation or miscommunication.

Communication skills are essential for game designers as they enable effective collaboration, convey design ideas, facilitate feedback and iteration, bridge artistic and technical perspectives, present ideas to stakeholders, resolve conflicts, and document design concepts. By honing their communication skills, game designers can foster a cohesive and collaborative development environment, ensuring that their design vision is effectively translated into a successful and engaging game.

Why are collaboration skills essential for a games designer?

Collaboration skills are essential for game designers because game development is a highly collaborative process that involves working with diverse teams and individuals.

Here are some reasons why collaboration skills are crucial for game designers:

Teamwork and Integration: Game designers collaborate with artists, programmers, sound designers, and other professionals to bring their design vision to life. Effective collaboration skills allow designers to work harmoniously with team members, integrate different elements seamlessly, and ensure that the overall game design aligns with the project's goals.

Shared Vision and Communication: Effective collaboration relies on shared vision and clear communication. When game designers collaborate with their team members, they must possess strong collaboration skills to effectively express their design concepts, actively listen to others' perspectives, and foster a collective vision for the game. This ensures that everyone is aligned and working together towards a common objective.

Leveraging Diverse Expertise: Collaboration allows game designers to leverage the diverse expertise and skills of their team members. Each individual brings a unique set of insights and knowledge to the table, and the collaboration skills of designers enable them to harness this collective expertise. They can tap into the strengths of others, incorporate diverse viewpoints, and cultivate a more comprehensive and innovative game design. By embracing collaboration, game designers create an environment where the collective intelligence and varied skillsets of the team contribute to a more well-rounded and exceptional game.

Problem-solving and Creativity: Collaborating with others enhances problem-solving and creativity. Through collaboration, designers can brainstorm ideas, bounce concepts off one another, and collectively find innovative solutions to design challenges. The diverse perspectives and collective intelligence of the team can lead to more robust and creative game design solutions.

Iterative Design and Feedback: Collaboration plays a crucial role in the iterative design process. Designers rely on feedback from team members to refine and improve their designs. Collaborative skills allow designers to receive and provide constructive feedback, incorporate suggestions, and iterate on their designs effectively. This iterative process leads to the development of a higher quality and more polished game.

Conflict Resolution and Adaptability: Collaboration skills enable designers to navigate conflicts or disagreements that may arise during the development process. Designers must be adaptable, open to compromise, and capable of finding solutions that accommodate different viewpoints. Strong collaboration skills foster a positive and supportive work environment, ensuring that conflicts are resolved effectively and that the project can progress smoothly.

Collaboration skills are essential for game designers as they enable effective teamwork, communication, and integration of ideas. Collaboration allows designers to leverage the expertise of others, enhance problem-solving and creativity, iterate on designs through feedback, and navigate conflicts. By cultivating strong collaboration skills, game designers can create exceptional games that benefit from the collective efforts and talents of the entire team.

Why do games designers need to understand player experiences?

Understanding player experience is crucial for game designers because it forms the foundation for creating enjoyable and engaging games.

Here are some reasons why skills in understanding player experience are essential for game designers:

Player-Centric Design: Game designers need to put themselves in the players' shoes and consider how they will interact with the game. By understanding player experience, designers can create games that resonate with the target audience, meet their expectations, and provide a satisfying and immersive gameplay experience.

Player Engagement and Retention: Designers with a strong understanding of player experience can create games that captivate and retain players. They can identify what motivates players, what keeps them engaged, and what factors contribute to a positive experience. This knowledge allows designers to craft gameplay mechanics, challenges, and rewards that keep players coming back for more.

Emotional Impact: The emotional impact of games is truly extraordinary, as they have the power to elicit a myriad of emotions from players, ranging from exhilaration to empathy. With a profound understanding of player experience, game designers can purposefully imbue game elements, narratives, and aesthetics that evoke precise emotions, intensifying the emotional resonance and nurturing a profound and meaningful bond between players and the game world.

Through careful craftsmanship, designers can create experiences that evoke joy, suspense, sorrow, triumph, and a host of other emotions, leaving a lasting impression on players and forging a deep connection that transcends the virtual realm.

Usability and Accessibility: Designers with an understanding of player experience can create games that are user-friendly and accessible to a wide range of players. They consider factors such as intuitive controls, clear instructions, and inclusive design principles to ensure that players can easily navigate and enjoy the game without barriers.

Iterative Design and Testing: Understanding player experience allows designers to iterate on their designs based on player feedback and testing. They can analyze player behavior, preferences, and frustrations to make informed adjustments and improvements. This iterative design process, driven by an understanding of player experience, leads to the refinement of game mechanics, levels, and overall gameplay.

Market Relevance: In today's fiercely competitive gaming industry, staying attuned to player experience is of utmost importance to create games that deeply resonate with the market. Game designers who possess a keen awareness of player preferences, emerging trends, and technological advancements have the ability to develop games that cater to the ever-evolving needs and desires of players.

By aligning their creations with the pulse of the gaming community, designers can position their games as relevant, appealing, and highly sought-after in a dynamic marketplace. This acute market relevance not only enhances the commercial success of the games but also establishes a strong bond between players and the brand, fostering loyalty and a sense of connection that fuels ongoing engagement and enthusiastic support.

Also, honing their skills in understanding player experience, game designers can create games that are engaging, emotionally impactful, accessible, and relevant to their target audience. This focus on player experience forms the cornerstone of successful game design and ensures that players have an immersive and enjoyable experience with the games they play.

Why are adaptability skills essential for a games designer?

Adaptability is a vital skill for game designers, given the dynamic nature of the gaming industry and the ever-evolving demands of players.

Here are a few compelling reasons why adaptability skills are essential for game designers:

Embracing Technological Advancements: The gaming industry is constantly propelled forward by advancements in technology. As a game designer, being adaptable allows you to embrace and harness new tools, platforms, and technologies that emerge. By staying abreast of technological advancements, you can create innovative and ground-breaking gaming experiences that push the boundaries of what is possible.

Responding to Changing Player Expectations: Players' preferences and expectations are subject to change over time. Being adaptable enables game designers to understand and respond to these shifts, ensuring that their games remain relevant and engaging. By adapting to changing player expectations, you can deliver experiences that resonate deeply with your target audience and keep them captivated.

Navigating Industry Trends: The gaming industry is influenced by trends in game design, mechanics, and aesthetics. By being adaptable, game designers can keep a finger on the pulse of industry trends and adapt their design approaches accordingly. This allows you to create games that align with current market demands, increasing their appeal and commercial viability.

Flexibility in Design Iteration: Game development involves an iterative process of testing, feedback, and refinement. Being adaptable enables designers to embrace feedback and make necessary adjustments to their designs. It allows you to iterate and refine your ideas based on player insights, ensuring that the final product delivers an exceptional gaming experience.

Collaborative Agility: Game development is a collaborative endeavor that requires effective teamwork and communication. Adaptability allows game designers to collaborate seamlessly with diverse team members, including artists, programmers, and sound designers. By being adaptable in your approach, you can readily adapt to different perspectives, incorporate input from others, and foster a cohesive and harmonious team dynamic.

Thriving in Project Constraints: Game designers often work within project constraints, such as limited resources, tight schedules, or technical limitations. Being adaptable enables you to navigate these constraints creatively, finding innovative solutions and making the most of available resources. It empowers you to adapt your design vision to fit the project's parameters without compromising the quality of the game.

Adaptability is a critical skill for game designers as it enables them to embrace technological advancements, respond to changing player expectations, navigate industry trends, iterate effectively, collaborate seamlessly, and thrive within project constraints. By being adaptable, game designers can stay ahead of the curve and create remarkable gaming experiences that captivate players and push the boundaries of the medium.

Why is attention to detail skills essential for a games designer?

Attention to detail is an indispensable skill for game designers due to its significant impact on the quality and polish of the final game.

Here are several reasons why attention to detail skills are essential for game designers:

Game World Immersion: Games thrive on creating immersive and believable worlds for players to explore. Attention to detail allows designers to meticulously craft every aspect of the game world, including environments, objects, characters, and animations. By paying close attention to even the smallest elements, game designers can enhance the player's immersion and create a cohesive and engaging experience.

Gameplay Balance and Mechanics: Balancing gameplay mechanics is crucial for ensuring an enjoyable and fair experience for players. Attention to detail enables designers to fine-tune gameplay elements such as difficulty levels, character abilities, item attributes, and progression systems. By meticulously analyzing and adjusting these aspects, game designers can create a balanced and satisfying gameplay experience.

Visual and Audio Fidelity: Details in visual and audio design significantly contribute to the overall quality and aesthetics of a game. Game designers with strong attention to detail can carefully consider lighting, textures, sound effects, music, and voice acting to create a rich and immersive audiovisual experience. By ensuring consistency and precision in these elements, designers can elevate the game's overall presentation.

Bug Fixing and Quality Assurance: Attention to detail is crucial during the bug fixing and quality assurance stages of game development. Game designers need to carefully identify and address any issues or glitches that may arise during testing. By paying close attention to player feedback and thoroughly testing the game, designers can spot and rectify even the most minor bugs or inconsistencies, resulting in a polished and seamless gameplay experience.

Storytelling and Narrative: Attention to detail plays a significant role in storytelling and narrative design. Game designers need to meticulously plan and structure the narrative elements of the game, including plot twists, character development, dialogue, and world-building details. By being attentive to narrative continuity and consistency, designers can create a captivating and coherent story that resonates with players.

User Interface and User Experience (UI/UX): User Interface (UI) and User Experience (UX) are pivotal components of game design, heavily influencing player engagement and satisfaction. Meticulous attention to detail empowers designers to craft interfaces that are intuitive, visually captivating, and effortlessly navigable. By focusing on user interaction and carefully refining the UI/UX elements, designers can cultivate a seamless and delightful gaming experience, where players can effortlessly access information, perform actions, and immerse themselves in the game's world.

Attention to detail is essential for game designers as it ensures the creation of immersive game worlds, balanced gameplay mechanics, visually and audibly appealing experiences, bug-free games, compelling narratives, and user-friendly interfaces. By cultivating a keen eye for detail, game designers can elevate the overall quality of their games and deliver exceptional experiences that resonate with players.

Why do games designers need a passion for video games?

Having a passion for video games is not necessarily a skill but rather a characteristic that greatly benefits game designers in their work.

Here are a few reasons why having a passion for video games is important for game designers:

Intrinsic Motivation: A genuine passion for video games serves as a powerful intrinsic motivator for game designers. It fuels their drive to create captivating and immersive experiences, pushing them to go above and beyond in their work. Designing games is not just a job for them; it is a labor of love driven by their deep appreciation for the medium.

Understanding Player Perspective: Being passionate about video games allows designers to understand the perspective of players more intimately. They have firsthand experience as players themselves, enabling them to empathize with their target audience. This understanding helps them design games that resonate with players, cater to their preferences, and deliver the kind of experiences they enjoy.

Staying Informed and Inspired: Passionate game designers tend to immerse themselves in the world of video games, constantly staying informed about industry trends, emerging technologies, and new game releases. Their passion drives them to explore and play a wide variety of games, which in turn inspires them with fresh ideas and innovative approaches in their own designs.

Advocating for Player Experience: Game designers who have a passion for video games are often passionate advocates for the player experience. They prioritize creating enjoyable, immersive, and memorable experiences for players above all else. Their passion drives them to go the extra mile in refining gameplay mechanics, balancing difficulty levels, and ensuring the overall quality of the game, all with the player's enjoyment in mind.

Persistence and Resilience: The game development process can be challenging and demanding, requiring dedication, perseverance, and the ability to overcome obstacles. Passionate game designers are more likely to possess the resilience and determination needed to overcome setbacks, iterate on designs, and bring their vision to fruition.

While having a passion for video games is not a skill that can be learned or acquired, it is a valuable characteristic that fuels a designer's creativity, understanding of player perspectives, and commitment to delivering exceptional gaming experiences.

Chapter 2 - The Conceptual Phase

The initial stage of game design, known as the conceptual phase, serves as the cornerstone for creating a game. It encompasses the generation and exploration of ideas, concepts, and overarching themes that will shape the game's design. During this phase, game designers concentrate on defining the fundamental aspects of the game, such as its genre, gameplay mechanics, narrative, visual style, and target audience.

Within the conceptual phase, designers engage in brainstorming, research, and creative discussions to establish a clear vision for the game. They may produce concept art, write design documents, or develop prototypes to delve into and refine their ideas. This phase is characterized by experimentation and iteration as designers explore different possibilities and assess their feasibility.

The conceptual phase holds immense importance as it lays the groundwork for the entire game development process. It establishes the game's identity, guiding the subsequent design and development stages. The decisions made during this phase exert a significant influence on the overall player experience and shape the final product.

Collaboration and feedback from diverse stakeholders, including other members of the development team, play a vital role in the conceptual phase. This ensures that the vision aligns with the project's objectives and limitations. Striking a balance between creative thinking, critical analysis, and practical considerations is essential to create a strong foundation for the game's design.

The importance of ideation and brainstorming

Ideation and brainstorming are essential components of the game design process, playing a pivotal role in shaping innovative and engaging gaming experiences.

Here are some key reasons why ideation and brainstorming are of utmost importance in game design:

Generating Fresh Ideas: Ideation and brainstorming provide a platform for game designers to generate a multitude of fresh and original ideas. By encouraging divergent thinking and exploring various possibilities, designers can break free from conventional approaches and discover innovative concepts that set their games apart. This creative exploration allows for the development of unique gameplay mechanics, compelling narratives, and immersive worlds.

Fostering Collaboration and Synergy: Brainstorming sessions bring together designers, artists, programmers, and other team members, fostering collaboration and synergy. Through open and inclusive discussions, team members can share their perspectives, build upon each other's ideas, and create a shared vision for the game. Collaboration allows for the pooling of diverse expertise, leading to more refined and well-rounded game designs.

Overcoming Design Challenges: Ideation and brainstorming are powerful tools for overcoming design challenges. By collectively addressing obstacles and brainstorming potential solutions, designers can tap into the collective intelligence of the team. This collaborative problem-solving approach allows for the identification of innovative design solutions that may not have been apparent through individual efforts alone.

Encouraging Iterative Design: Ideation and brainstorming support the iterative nature of game design. Through multiple rounds of ideation and brainstorming, designers can continuously refine and iterate on their ideas. This iterative process allows for the exploration of different design possibilities, the refinement of gameplay mechanics, and the enhancement of the overall player experience.

Sparking Innovation and Pushing Boundaries: Ideation and brainstorming push the boundaries of creativity in game design. By encouraging designers to think beyond established norms and explore uncharted territories, these processes fuel innovation. They inspire designers to experiment with new mechanics, technologies, and design approaches, resulting in games that offer fresh and exciting experiences to players.

Enhancing Player Engagement: Ideation and brainstorming directly contribute to enhancing player engagement. By carefully considering the desires, preferences, and expectations of the target audience during these processes, designers can create games that resonate with players. Through innovative ideas and captivating concepts, designers can craft gameplay experiences that captivate players and keep them immersed in the game world.

Encouraging Continued Growth and Learning: Ideation and brainstorming foster an environment of continuous growth and learning for game designers. By engaging in these processes, designers are exposed to new ideas, perspectives, and approaches. This exposure encourages them to expand their knowledge, explore emerging trends, and stay updated with the latest advancements in the gaming industry.

Ideation and brainstorming are critical components of game design, enabling designers to generate fresh ideas, foster collaboration, overcome design challenges, spark innovation, and enhance player engagement. By embracing these processes, game designers can create extraordinary gaming experiences that leave a lasting impact on players and contribute to the evolution of the gaming industry.

Researching market trends and player preferences

In the vast realm of game design, one key element reigns supreme: understanding market trends and player preferences. It is the compass that guides designers through the ever-shifting landscape of gaming, enabling them to navigate the currents of player demands and industry dynamics. Researching market trends unveils the hidden patterns and emerging forces that shape the gaming world, while delving into player preferences unlocks the secrets of player desires and motivations.

Researching market trends and player preferences is crucial in game design for several reasons:

Meeting Player Expectations: Understanding market trends and player preferences allows game designers to create experiences that align with what players are seeking. By staying informed about the latest trends, preferences, and demands of the target audience, designers can tailor their games to meet player expectations. This increases the likelihood of attracting and retaining a dedicated player base.

Identifying Opportunities: Researching market trends helps designers identify potential gaps or under served niches in the gaming market. By uncovering emerging trends, genres, or gameplay mechanics, designers can capitalize on opportunities to create innovative and unique games that cater to specific player preferences. This can lead to increased market visibility and a competitive advantage.

Enhancing Player Engagement: Understanding player preferences allows designers to create games that engage players on a deeper level. By incorporating features, mechanics, and storytelling elements that resonate with the target audience, designers can craft immersive experiences that captivate and hold players' attention. This leads to increased player satisfaction, higher engagement levels, and potentially greater success for the game.

Optimizing Monetization Strategies: Researching player preferences helps designers make informed decisions about monetization strategies. By understanding what players are willing to pay for and their attitudes towards different monetization models, designers can implement effective and player-friendly monetization strategies. This ensures a fair balance between revenue generation and player satisfaction, contributing to the long-term success and sustainability of the game.

Minimizing Risk: Market research helps designers mitigate the risks associated with game development. By studying market trends and player preferences, designers can make informed decisions about game concepts, features, and design choices. This reduces the likelihood of developing a game that does not resonate with the target audience, minimizing the risk of poor reception or commercial failure.

Staying Competitive: The gaming industry is highly competitive, and staying informed about market trends and player preferences is essential for designers to remain competitive. By understanding what other games are successful and what players are gravitating towards, designers can continuously improve their designs, differentiate themselves from competitors, and offer unique experiences that stand out in the market.

Researching market trends and player preferences empowers

game designers to create games that resonate with the target audience, deliver engaging experiences, and increase the chances of success in a competitive industry. It helps designers make informed decisions, optimize their designs, and ultimately create games that captivate and satisfy players.

Developing a unique game concept and vision

Developing a unique game concept and vision is a fundamental task for game designers. It involves harnessing their creativity and imagination to craft an original and captivating idea that sets their game apart. By exploring various sources of inspiration, defining core mechanics, and establishing the game world, designers breathe life into their vision.

Through an iterative design process and an emphasis on innovation, they refine their concept to create an immersive and unforgettable experience. By aligning their vision with the practical constraints of development, designers ensure that their unique concept can be brought to life within the given resources. Ultimately, the goal is to create a game that not only stands out in a crowded industry but also resonates with players, leaving a lasting impact.

Here are some key steps and considerations they take:

Creative Exploration: Game designers engage in brainstorming sessions, creative exercises, and research to explore a wide range of concepts and inspirations. They draw from diverse sources such as literature, movies, art, history, and other games to spark their imagination and uncover unique ideas.

Defining Core Mechanics: Designers identify the core mechanics and gameplay elements that will define the essence of the game. They consider factors such as player interactions, challenges, progression systems, and rewards. These mechanics form the foundation upon which the entire game experience will be built.

Establishing the Game World: Game designers craft the world in which the game will be set, defining its lore, setting, atmosphere, and visual style. They create a cohesive and immersive universe that aligns with the game's vision and resonates with players.

Iterative Design: Game designers understand that developing a unique concept requires iterative refinement. They prototype and playtest early versions of the game to gather feedback, evaluate the effectiveness of the mechanics, and iterate on the concept. This iterative process allows them to fine-tune and polish their ideas, ensuring the game's uniqueness and playability.

Emphasizing Innovation: Game designers strive to bring innovation to their concept, whether through novel mechanics, inventive storytelling, unique art styles, or ground breaking technology. They aim to push the boundaries of what has been done before, creating experiences that captivate players and stand out in the competitive gaming landscape.

Aligning Vision and Constraints: Designers must consider the constraints and limitations of the development process, including budget, time, and available resources. They balance their creative vision with practical considerations, ensuring that the concept can be feasibly developed within the given constraints.

During this exciting journey, game designers constantly polish their concept and vision, aiming to create an experience that is not only one-of-a-kind but also deeply connects with the intended audience. They wholeheartedly embrace creativity, exploration, and innovation, pouring their passion into crafting games that leave an indelible mark on players and the entire industry.

Creating a compelling narrative or gameplay

hook

Creating a compelling narrative or gameplay hook is a multifaceted process that requires games designers to tap into their creative prowess and storytelling abilities. To create a captivating narrative, designers delve into the realms of character development, world-building, and plot construction. They craft memorable characters with distinct personalities, motivations, and conflicts, allowing players to form emotional connections and engage with the story on a deeper level. By carefully structuring the game's plot, designers create tension, suspense, and moments of excitement, ensuring a satisfying narrative arc.

In addition to narrative-driven games, gameplay-driven games also rely on a strong gameplay hook to captivate players. Designers focus on developing innovative and engaging mechanics that offer unique and compelling gameplay experiences. They experiment with different gameplay elements, such as combat systems, puzzle mechanics, or exploration mechanics, seeking to create a sense of challenge, discovery, and mastery. By striking the right balance between difficulty and reward, designers ensure that players are constantly motivated to progress and explore.

To create a compelling narrative or gameplay hook, games designers often draw inspiration from a variety of sources, including literature, movies, real-life events, and cultural references. They analyze market trends, player preferences, and the competitive landscape to identify opportunities for innovation and differentiation. Through brainstorming sessions, prototyping, and playtesting, designers refine their ideas, iterate on gameplay mechanics, and fine-tune narrative elements.

Furthermore, creating a compelling narrative or gameplay hook requires designers to consider the target audience and tailor the experience to their preferences. They conduct user research, collect feedback, and iterate on their designs to ensure that the game resonates with players and keeps them engaged throughout the gameplay experience.

Ultimately, the goal of creating a compelling narrative or gameplay hook is to immerse players in a captivating world, evoke their emotions, and provide a memorable and enjoyable gaming experience. It is the combination of engaging storytelling, innovative mechanics, and player-centric design that sets games apart and leaves a lasting impact on players.

Chapter 3 - Pre-production: Planning and Documentation

In game design, the pre-production phase is a crucial stage that involves extensive planning and documentation to lay the foundation for the game's development. During this phase, game designers collaborate with the development team to define the project's scope, goals, and requirements. Planning and documentation play a vital role in shaping the direction of the game and ensuring a smooth development process.

One key aspect of pre-production is the creation of a game design document (GDD). The GDD serves as a comprehensive blueprint that outlines the game's concept, mechanics, characters, levels, and overall vision. It provides a central reference point for the entire team, ensuring everyone is aligned and working towards a common goal. The GDD includes detailed descriptions of gameplay features, art style, audio design, and any technical considerations.

Additionally, pre-production involves conducting thorough research and analysis. This includes market research to understand player preferences, trends, and competition. It also involves gathering reference materials, studying similar games, and conducting feasibility studies to assess technical constraints and resource requirements.

During the pre-production phase, game designers also work on prototyping and iteration. Prototypes are essential for testing and refining gameplay mechanics, level designs, and user interfaces. They allow designers to experiment with ideas, gather feedback, and make necessary adjustments before entering full production.

Furthermore, pre-production includes establishing project timelines, milestones, and resource allocation. This phase requires careful project management to ensure that the development process stays on track and meets deadlines. It involves coordinating with artists, programmers, sound designers, and other team members to create a well-defined production plan.

Overall, the pre-production phase in game design is a critical step in the development process. It involves meticulous planning, thorough documentation, and effective communication to set the stage for a successful and cohesive game development journey. By investing time and effort into pre-production, game designers can minimize risks, streamline workflows, and pave the way for a smooth transition into full production.

Building the game design document (GDD)

The game design document (GDD) is a comprehensive and detailed document that serves as a blueprint for the game's development. It is an essential tool for game designers as it outlines the vision, mechanics, features, and overall structure of the game. The GDD acts as a central reference point that guides the entire development team throughout the production process.

For game designers, the GDD is a crucial document that captures their creative ideas and translates them into a tangible plan. It allows them to articulate their vision for the game, define its gameplay mechanics, describe the characters and world, and establish the narrative or storyline. The GDD helps game designers to communicate their concepts effectively to the rest of the team, ensuring a shared understanding of the game's direction.

The GDD typically includes various sections such as:

Overview: Provides a high-level summary of the game, including its genre, target audience, and key features.

Gameplay: Describes the core mechanics, controls, objectives, and progression systems that drive the gameplay experience.

Characters and Story: Introduces the main characters, their motivations, and their roles within the game's narrative. It outlines the overall storyline, plot points, and any branching or alternative paths.

Levels and Environments: Defines the different levels, environments, and settings within the game. It describes the layout, obstacles, puzzles, and interactive elements of each level.

Art and Visuals: Outlines the art style, aesthetics, and visual direction for the game. It may include concept art, reference images, and guidelines for character design, environments, and visual effects.

Audio and Sound Design: Specifies the audio elements such as music, sound effects, voiceovers, and how they contribute to the overall game experience.

Technical Considerations: Includes technical requirements, platform-specific considerations, performance optimization, and any limitations or constraints that need to be considered during development.

The GDD serves as a living document that evolves and gets updated throughout the game's development cycle. It acts as a reference for the team members involved in different disciplines, including artists, programmers, sound designers, and producers. The GDD helps ensure that the entire team remains aligned with the game's vision and goals, enabling a cohesive and focused development process.

The game design document is a vital tool for game designers as it allows them to articulate their creative ideas, define the game's mechanics and features, and provide guidance for the development team. It serves as a roadmap that aligns the team's efforts and ensures a consistent vision for the game.

Here's an example of an extremely simplified game design document for a hypothetical action-adventure game:

=== Overview ===
Game Title: "Mystic Quest"
Genre: Action-Adventure
Target Audience: Players aged 12 and above
Key Features: Exploration, puzzle-solving, combat, character progression

=== Gameplay ===
Core Mechanics: Third-person exploration and combat,

puzzle-solving, platforming
Controls: Standard gamepad controls with intuitive button mapping
Objectives: Players must navigate through a series of interconnected levels, defeat enemies, solve puzzles, and collect items to progress.

=== Characters and Story ===
Protagonist: Name - Aiden, a young adventurer with a mysterious background
Antagonist: Name - Lord Malachi, an evil sorcerer seeking ancient artefacts for his dark plans
Storyline: Aiden embarks on a quest to thwart Lord Malachi's plans and save the world from impending doom. Along the way, Aiden discovers his own hidden powers and unravels secrets about his past.

=== Levels and Environments ===
Level 1: Ancient Ruins
Description: A sprawling, overgrown ruin filled with traps, puzzles, and hidden chambers.
Objectives: Retrieve the artefact hidden within the ruins while overcoming environmental hazards and solving puzzles.
Key Features: Explorable areas, crumbling platforms, ancient mechanisms.

Level 2: Enchanted Forest
Description: A lush forest teeming with magical creatures and mystical phenomena.
Objectives: Navigate through the forest, overcome guardian creatures, and find the hidden entrance to the next area.
Key Features: Dense foliage, interactive wildlife, environmental hazards.

=== Art and Visuals ===
Art Style: Realistic with a touch of fantasy elements
Character Design: Aiden as a brave and agile adventurer, Lord Malachi as a menacing sorcerer
Environments: Richly detailed ruins, vibrant and diverse forest

with magical lighting effects.

=== Audio and Sound Design ===
Background Music: Epic and atmospheric tracks to enhance the mood and immerse players in the game world
Sound Effects: Engaging and realistic sounds for combat, environmental interactions, and puzzle-solving
Voice-overs: Key characters have voice-overs for dialogues and important narrative moments.

=== Technical Considerations ===
Platforms: PlayStation 5, Xbox Series X, PC
Performance Optimization: Targeting a stable frame rate of 60 FPS, optimized loading times, and efficient memory usage.
Limitations: The game should be playable with a wide range of controller setups, taking into account accessibility options.

Just a friendly heads-up, this example is a simplified one. In real game development, a game design document would usually be way more detailed and specific. It's crafted to perfectly fit the unique requirements and scope of the project. So, keep in mind that there's a lot more to it than what meets the eye!

Does the game design document during production of a game?

Yes, the game design document often undergoes changes and revisions throughout the development of a game. As the development progresses, new ideas may emerge, technical limitations may arise, and player feedback may influence the direction of the game. These factors can lead to updates and adjustments to the game design document.

The iterative nature of game development encourages flexibility and adaptation. Game designers continuously evaluate the design document, gather feedback from the development team and playtesting sessions, and make necessary revisions to improve the game's quality and align it with the evolving vision. These changes can include refining gameplay mechanics, adjusting level designs, modifying story elements, or enhancing visual and audio aspects.

The game design document serves as a living document that evolves alongside the game's development. It acts as a reference point and communication tool for the development team, ensuring that everyone remains aligned with the overall vision and goals of the game. By adapting and updating the game design document as needed, designers can navigate the dynamic nature of game development and create a better end product.

Outlining game mechanics, systems, and progression

Games designers outline game mechanics, systems, and progression for a computer game through a systematic and iterative process.

Here are the key steps involved:

Conceptualization: The designer begins by conceptualizing the core gameplay mechanics and systems that will drive the game experience. This involves brainstorming ideas, exploring innovative concepts, and considering how these elements will interact to create engaging gameplay.

Defining Game Mechanics: The designer identifies and outlines the specific mechanics that will shape player interaction within the game. This includes determining the player's abilities, the rules governing the game world, and the various actions and interactions available to the player.

Balancing and Tuning: The designer focuses on balancing the game mechanics to ensure a satisfying and fair gameplay experience. This involves adjusting variables such as player attributes, enemy difficulty, resource management, and progression pacing to create an optimal level of challenge and reward.

Progression and Rewards: The designer outlines the game's progression system, which includes determining the player's goals, milestones, and the rewards they will receive for achieving them. This can include unlocking new levels, abilities, items, or story elements to maintain player engagement and provide a sense of accomplishment.

Iterative Testing and Refinement: The designer conducts playtesting sessions to gather feedback and evaluate the effectiveness of the outlined mechanics, systems, and progression. Based on player feedback and observations, adjustments are made to enhance gameplay, address imbalances, and ensure a rewarding player experience.

Throughout this process, designers consider factors such as player motivation, skill progression, balance between challenge and accessibility, and the overall player experience. They aim to create a cohesive and engaging gameplay loop that keeps players immersed, motivated, and eager to progress through the game.

Defining a games mechanics

Game designers use various techniques to define a game's mechanics, ensuring they are well-structured and aligned with the intended gameplay experience.

Here are some commonly employed techniques:

System Mapping: Designers create visual diagrams or flowcharts to map out the interconnections between different gameplay systems. This helps in identifying relationships, dependencies, and interactions among mechanics, allowing for a comprehensive understanding of how they contribute to the overall gameplay.

System mapping is a technique used by game designers to visually represent the relationships and interactions between different gameplay systems in a game. It involves creating diagrams or flowcharts that illustrate how various mechanics, subsystems, and components connect and influence each other.

The process of system mapping begins by identifying the major gameplay systems present in the game. These systems can include combat, exploration, puzzle-solving, character progression, economy, and more. Each system is then broken down into its individual components, such as actions, rules, variables, and feedback loops.

The designer maps out the connections and dependencies between these components, showcasing how they interact and impact one another. Arrows, lines, or connectors are used to indicate the flow of information, resources, or actions between different components. This visual representation allows the designer to see the intricate web of relationships within the game's mechanics.

System mapping helps designers gain a holistic view of the game's structure and balance. It enables them to analyze the potential consequences of changes made to one system on the rest of the game. By identifying dependencies and potential conflicts early on, designers can make informed decisions and ensure a cohesive and enjoyable gameplay experience.

Furthermore, system mapping aids in identifying emergent gameplay possibilities. It allows designers to see how the combination or interaction of different systems can create new and unexpected experiences. This can lead to innovative gameplay mechanics or unique player strategies that enhance the depth and replayability of the game.

System mapping also serves as a valuable communication tool within the development team. It helps designers effectively convey their ideas to artists, programmers, and other team members, ensuring a shared understanding of the game's mechanics and facilitating collaboration.

Overall, system mapping is a powerful technique that enables game designers to visualize and analyze the intricate relationships between gameplay systems. It helps them create well-structured and balanced mechanics, anticipate the impact of changes, and foster creativity and innovation within the game design process.

Prototyping: Designers build early versions of the game or specific gameplay mechanics to test and iterate upon. Prototyping allows them to experiment with different ideas, observe how mechanics work in practice, and gather feedback from playtesters. This iterative process helps refine and solidify the mechanics based on player engagement and enjoyment.

Prototyping is a crucial process in game design that involves creating early, simplified versions of a game to test and iterate on gameplay mechanics, interactions, and overall player experience. It is an essential step in the iterative design cycle and allows designers to explore ideas, validate concepts, and make informed decisions before investing significant resources into full-scale development.

The process of prototyping typically starts with the identification of the core gameplay mechanics and features that the designer wants to test. These could include movement, combat, puzzle-solving, level progression, or any other key elements that define the game experience. The focus at this stage is to capture the essence of the gameplay and create a playable representation of the concept.

Prototypes can take various forms depending on the complexity and scope of the game. They can range from paper prototypes, which use sketches, cutouts, or simple props, to digital prototypes created with game development tools or specialized prototyping software. The key is to create a functional representation that allows for interaction and evaluation of the gameplay.

The primary purpose of prototyping is to gather feedback and evaluate the design's strengths and weaknesses. Playtesting is an integral part of the prototyping process, where designers observe and gather data from players engaging with the prototype. This feedback helps identify areas that need improvement, discover potential design flaws, and gain insights into the player's experience.

Through prototyping, designers can experiment, iterate, and refine their ideas. They can test different variations of mechanics, explore alternative approaches, and assess the impact of changes on the overall gameplay. Prototyping also provides an opportunity to identify technical challenges, usability issues, and any potential limitations early in the development process.

Prototypes serve as a communication tool between designers, developers, artists, and other stakeholders involved in the game's production. They help convey design intentions and facilitate discussions about the game's direction. Additionally, prototypes can be used to secure funding, attract publishers, or gather interest from potential players, as they provide a tangible representation of the game's potential.

It's important to note that prototypes are not meant to be polished or final versions of the game. They are iterative in nature and are expected to evolve based on the learnings and insights gained during the prototyping phase. The goal is to validate ideas, experiment with mechanics, and refine the design to create a solid foundation for further development.

In summary, prototyping is a vital aspect of game design that allows designers to test and refine gameplay mechanics, interactions, and player experience. It provides an opportunity to gather feedback, make informed design decisions, identify challenges, and iterate on the game's core elements. Through prototyping, designers can shape and evolve their concepts into engaging and compelling experiences for players.

Mechanics Documentation: Designers write detailed documentation that outlines each game mechanic, including its purpose, rules, interactions, and potential variations. This documentation serves as a reference for the development team, ensuring a clear and consistent understanding of the intended mechanics throughout the production process.

Mechanics documentation is an essential process in game design where we capture and provide detailed information about the different gameplay mechanics and systems that will be present in the game. Its purpose is to serve as a comprehensive reference and guide for the development team, making sure that everyone involved understands how the game mechanics function and interact with each other.

Our mechanics documentation ensures that the gameplay experience is consistent, coherent, and well-balanced. We start by identifying the core mechanics that drive the gameplay, such as movement, combat, puzzles, and resource management. Each mechanic is then described in depth, including its purpose, rules, inputs, outputs, and any dependencies or constraints that are relevant.

To make it even more intuitive, we may include diagrams or visual representations to illustrate how different mechanics flow and interact with one another. These visuals help the development team better grasp the relationships and contributions of each mechanic to the overall game experience.

In addition to describing individual mechanics, our documentation covers how these mechanics work together harmoniously to create an engaging gameplay experience. We explain how they synergize, complement, or build upon each other to add depth and variety.

Anticipating different player actions or choices, our mechanics documentation also addresses potential edge cases, exceptions, and special scenarios that may arise during gameplay. This ensures that the mechanics can handle various player interactions while remaining robust and balanced.

Furthermore, our documentation includes guidelines and best practices for implementing and fine-tuning the mechanics. This information assists programmers, artists, and other members of the development team in understanding the technical requirements and considerations for effectively implementing the mechanics.

By serving as a communication tool, our documentation allows designers to effectively convey their ideas and intentions to the development team, fostering a shared understanding of the gameplay mechanics.

Throughout the development process, our mechanics documentation may evolve and be updated to reflect changes, improvements, or new additions to the game's mechanics. It is a living document that adapts to the iterative nature of game development.

In summary, mechanics documentation plays a vital role in game design, outlining and describing the various gameplay mechanics and systems. It serves as a comprehensive reference for the development team, ensuring consistency, clarity, and effective implementation of the game's mechanics. By documenting the mechanics, we maintain a cohesive vision and guide the team towards creating a rich and enjoyable gameplay experience.

Iterative Design: Designers employ an iterative approach, continuously refining and adjusting mechanics based on playtesting and feedback. They observe how players interact with the mechanics, identify areas of confusion or imbalance, and make appropriate modifications to enhance the gameplay experience.

Iterative design is a crucial process in game design that involves continuously refining and improving the game through a cycle of testing, feedback, and iteration. It is an iterative approach where designers create, evaluate, and refine game elements based on player feedback and data analysis.

The goal of iterative design is to enhance the overall gameplay experience by addressing issues, improving mechanics, and optimizing various aspects of the game. It allows designers to iterate on their ideas, experiment with different solutions, and make informed decisions based on real-world testing.

The iterative design process typically involves the following steps:

Design and Implementation: The initial design of the game is created, including mechanics, levels, characters, and other elements. These design ideas are then implemented in a playable prototype or a build of the game.

Playtesting: The game prototype is tested by a group of players or a target audience. Playtesting can be done in-house or through external playtesting sessions. The players' feedback and observations are collected, focusing on their experiences, challenges, preferences, and suggestions.

Feedback and Analysis: The feedback gathered from playtesting is carefully analyzed by the design team. This involves identifying patterns, trends, and common issues reported by players. The team also looks for positive aspects of the game that can be emphasized or expanded upon.

Iteration: Based on the feedback and analysis, the design team makes informed decisions on what aspects of the game need improvement or adjustment. They revise the design, mechanics, levels, or other elements to address the identified issues and enhance the gameplay experience.

Testing and Validation: The revised version of the game is tested again to evaluate the impact of the changes. This process helps the design team validate the effectiveness of their iterations and gather additional feedback for further improvements.

Repeat: The cycle of playtesting, feedback analysis, iteration, and retesting continues throughout the development process. The design team keeps refining the game based on the results of each iteration, continually improving and polishing the gameplay experience.

Iterative design offers several benefits to game designers.

It allows them to:

Identify and address gameplay issues: By continuously testing the game with real players, designers can uncover flaws, inconsistencies, or areas of confusion in the gameplay. This feedback-driven approach helps them identify and address issues early on, ensuring a smoother and more enjoyable experience for players.

Optimize game mechanics and balance: Through iterative design, designers can fine-tune game mechanics, balance challenges, and adjust difficulty levels based on player feedback. This process helps them create a more engaging and satisfying gameplay experience.

Validate design decisions: Iterative design provides designers with the opportunity to validate their design choices through player feedback. It helps them understand how players perceive and respond to various elements of the game, allowing for informed design decisions and adjustments.

Foster innovation and creativity: By embracing an iterative approach, designers can experiment with new ideas, take risks, and explore innovative concepts. They can test unconventional mechanics, gameplay structures, or narrative approaches, gaining insights and pushing the boundaries of game design.

Increase player engagement and retention: Through iterative design, designers can refine the game to enhance player engagement, improve pacing, and increase replay value. By addressing player preferences and expectations, they can create a game that captivates and retains the interest of the target audience.

Iterative design is a vital process in game design that involves continuously refining and improving the game based on player feedback and analysis. It allows designers to address issues, optimize mechanics, validate design decisions, foster innovation, and create an engaging gameplay experience. By embracing an iterative approach, designers can evolve their game towards its fullest potential, resulting in a polished and immersive player experience.

Comparative Analysis: Designers study existing games, especially those with similar mechanics or themes, to understand how they have implemented and balanced similar gameplay elements. This analysis helps in identifying best practices, potential pitfalls, and innovative approaches that can be applied to their own game.

Comparative analysis is an important technique used by game designers to evaluate and understand the strengths and weaknesses of their own game in relation to other existing games in the market. It involves examining and comparing different aspects of games, such as mechanics, aesthetics, narrative, player experience, and overall design, to gain insights and inspiration for their own game.

The process of comparative analysis typically involves

the following steps:

Identifying Reference Games: Game designers start by selecting a set of reference games that are relevant to their own game's genre, target audience, or design goals. These reference games can be both successful and influential titles or even lesser-known games that excel in specific aspects.

Analyzing Game Mechanics: The designers delve into the mechanics of the reference games to understand how they work, how different systems and elements interact, and how they contribute to the overall gameplay experience. This analysis helps identify innovative or effective mechanics that can be adapted or expanded upon in their own game.

Evaluating Player Experience: Comparative analysis involves examining the player experience in reference games, including elements such as pacing, difficulty, player agency, engagement, and satisfaction. Designers analyze how the games create immersion, evoke emotions, and deliver meaningful experiences to players.

Assessing Aesthetics and Presentation: The visual and audio aspects of reference games are examined to understand how they contribute to the overall atmosphere, storytelling, and player engagement. This analysis helps designers gain inspiration for creating captivating visuals, compelling sound design, and immersive environments in their own game.

Considering Narrative and Storytelling: If narrative is an important component of the game being designed, comparative analysis involves studying the storytelling techniques, character development, plot structures, and narrative arcs of reference games. This analysis helps designers identify effective narrative approaches and storytelling methods that resonate with players.

Extracting Lessons and Inspiration: Throughout the

comparative analysis, designers extract valuable lessons, insights, and inspiration from the reference games. They identify successful design choices, innovative solutions, or unique features that can be adapted or applied to their own game. This process helps spark creativity and guide the development of their game's unique identity.

The benefits of comparative analysis for game designers are significant:

Insights into Best Practices: By analyzing successful games, designers can gain insights into best practices and industry standards. They can understand what works well in certain genres or player experiences and use that knowledge to inform their own design decisions.

Identification of Unique Selling Points: Comparative analysis helps designers identify the unique aspects or features that set their game apart from others in the market. By understanding what makes other games successful, they can refine and emphasize the aspects that make their game stand out.

Inspiration for Innovation: By examining different games and their design approaches, designers can find inspiration for innovative ideas and novel solutions. They can adapt and combine existing concepts to create new and exciting gameplay experiences.

Avoiding Design Pitfalls: Analyzing the weaknesses or limitations of other games can help designers avoid common pitfalls or design flaws. They can learn from the mistakes of others and make informed choices to create a more polished and well-rounded game.

Understanding Player Expectations: Comparative analysis provides valuable insights into player preferences and expectations. By studying popular games, designers can understand what players enjoy and what aspects contribute to a satisfying gaming experience. This understanding allows them to align their own game's design with player expectations.

In summary, comparative analysis is a valuable technique used by game designers to evaluate and gain insights from existing games. It helps them understand game mechanics, evaluate player experience, explore aesthetics and presentation, consider narrative approaches, and extract valuable lessons and inspiration. By leveraging the strengths of successful games and learning from their weaknesses, designers can create unique, engaging, and well-crafted games that resonate with their target audience.

By utilizing these techniques, game designers can effectively define game mechanics, ensuring they are engaging, balanced, and aligned with the overall vision of the game.

Crafting the game's visual and audio style

Crafting the visual and audio style of a game is a crucial aspect of game design that contributes to the overall immersion and player experience. Game designers employ various techniques and processes to create a cohesive and engaging visual and audio style.

Here are some key steps involved in this process:

Art Direction: The game designer works closely with artists, art directors, and graphic designers to establish the art direction for the game. This involves defining the overall visual style, including the colour palette, art style (e.g., realistic, stylized, pixel art), and the level of detail. The art direction sets the tone and atmosphere of the game and ensures consistency in the visual elements throughout.

Concept Art and Mood Boards: Artists and designers create concept art and mood boards that visually depict the desired aesthetic and ambiance of the game. These serve as references and inspiration for the development team and help establish a shared vision for the game's visual style. Concept art helps define the look of characters, environments, props, and other visual elements.

Visual Design Guidelines: Designers create visual design guidelines or style guides that outline the specific design principles and rules to be followed throughout the game. These guidelines cover aspects such as typography, iconography, layout, UI/UX design, and other visual elements. They ensure consistency and coherence in the visual representation of the game across different platforms and devices.

3D Modelling and Texturing: In games that utilize 3D graphics, game designers work with 3D modellers and texture artists to create realistic or stylized 3D models of characters, objects, and environments. They define the desired level of detail, the materials and textures to be used, and the overall aesthetic of the 3D assets. This process involves creating and refining the 3D models and applying textures to bring them to life.

Sound Design: Game designers collaborate with sound designers and composers to develop the game's audio style. This includes creating and selecting appropriate sound effects, ambient sounds, music, and voice-over recordings. The sound design enhances the immersion and atmosphere of the game, and it plays a crucial role in conveying emotions, providing feedback to the player, and creating an engaging audio experience.

Iterative Process: Crafting the visual and audio style of a game often involves an iterative process. Game designers regularly review and provide feedback on the visual and audio elements to ensure they align with the intended style and atmosphere of the game. They work closely with artists, sound designers, and other team members to refine and polish the visuals and audio, making adjustments as needed to achieve the desired effect.

Player Feedback and Testing: Throughout the development process, game designers gather player feedback and conduct testing to assess the impact of the visual and audio style on the player experience. They analyze how players respond to the visuals, audio cues, and overall atmosphere of the game, making adjustments based on feedback to optimize the game's visual and audio design for maximum impact.

Crafting the game's visual and audio style requires a combination of artistic vision, collaboration, and a deep understanding of the game's theme, genre, and target audience. By working closely with artists, sound designers, and other team members, game designers can create a visual and audio experience that enhances gameplay, immerses players in the game world, and contributes to a memorable and engaging gaming experience.

Collaborating with other team members (artists, programmers, etc.)

Game designers collaborate with various team members throughout the game development process to bring their vision to life and ensure a cohesive and successful game.

Here are some key ways in which game designers collaborate with other team members:

Artists: Game designers work closely with artists to translate their design concepts into visual assets. They collaborate on aspects such as character and environment design, art style, colour palette, and overall visual direction. Designers provide artistic direction and feedback, while artists contribute their creativity and skills to bring the game's visuals to fruition.

Programmers: Collaboration with programmers is essential for implementing game mechanics, systems, and features. Game designers work with programmers to discuss the technical feasibility of their design ideas and provide specifications for how the game should function. They communicate the desired player interactions, rules, and behaviours, and collaborate to iterate on the gameplay until it aligns with the design vision.

Sound Designers/Musicians: Game designers collaborate with sound designers and musicians to create the game's audio experience. They communicate the desired mood, atmosphere, and emotions that the audio should convey. Designers provide guidance on the sound effects, music styles, and overall audio integration within the game. This collaboration ensures that the audio enhances the player experience and complements the visual and gameplay elements.

Producers/Project Managers: Game designers work closely with producers or project managers to coordinate and manage the development process. They collaborate on project timelines, resource allocation, and ensure that the design vision aligns with the project's goals and constraints. Designers provide input on development milestones, feature prioritization, and overall project scope.

Quality Assurance/Testers: Collaboration with quality assurance (QA) testers is crucial for identifying and addressing bugs, glitches, and gameplay issues. Game designers work with QA testers to gather feedback, test new features, and iterate on the design based on the testing results. They collaborate to ensure the game meets the desired quality standards and provides a smooth and enjoyable player experience.

Writers/Narrative Designers: In games with a strong narrative component, game designers collaborate with writers and narrative designers to create compelling storylines, characters, and dialogue. They work together to ensure that the gameplay mechanics and narrative elements integrate seamlessly and enhance the overall player experience.

Designers provide input on the narrative structure, pacing, and player choices, while writers contribute their storytelling expertise.

User Interface/User Experience (UI/UX) Designers:
Collaboration with UI/UX designers is essential for creating an intuitive and user-friendly interface. Game designers work with UI/UX designers to define the layout, navigation, and visual presentation of menus, HUD elements, and user interactions. They collaborate to ensure that the interface aligns with the overall design vision, enhances gameplay clarity, and provides a seamless user experience.

Effective collaboration with team members is crucial for game designers to bring their design ideas to fruition and create a cohesive and successful game. Clear communication, active participation in discussions, and a shared understanding of the design goals are key elements in fostering a collaborative and productive working environment.

Chapter 4: Prototyping and Iteration

Prototyping holds immense significance in the realm of game design, serving as a fundamental tool that allows designers to explore, refine, and validate their ideas. It plays a pivotal role throughout the development process, enabling designers to test gameplay mechanics, evaluate the player experience, and make informed design decisions.

One of the key benefits of prototyping is concept validation. By creating a prototype, designers can quickly assess the potential of their initial concepts and determine if they have the potential to be fun, engaging, and aligned with their design goals. It provides a tangible representation of the game idea, allowing designers to experience first-hand how the core mechanics play out and evaluate if the gameplay experience is compelling enough to pursue further.

Prototyping supports an iterative design process, which is crucial for refining and improving game concepts. Through iterative prototyping, designers can gather feedback from playtests, observe player reactions, and identify areas that need adjustment. This feedback-driven approach helps in fine-tuning the gameplay mechanics, adjusting difficulty levels, addressing usability issues, and enhancing the overall experience. By repeatedly refining the prototype, designers can gradually shape the game into a more polished and enjoyable form.

In addition to gathering player feedback, prototypes facilitate effective communication and collaboration among team members. A well-executed prototype serves as a tangible representation of design ideas, making it easier for designers to convey their vision to artists, programmers, and other stakeholders. It enables fruitful discussions and allows for a shared understanding of the gameplay mechanics, visual style, and overall game concept. The collaborative environment encourages valuable contributions from different team members, resulting in a more cohesive and well-rounded game.

Prototyping also plays a crucial role in mitigating risks associated with game development. By creating a prototype, designers can identify and address potential problems or challenges early in the process. They can test the technical feasibility of their ideas, evaluate resource requirements, and assess the viability of design decisions. This proactive approach helps in minimizing the likelihood of costly mistakes or design flaws that could arise later in the development cycle.

Furthermore, prototypes are instrumental in pitching game concepts to publishers, investors, or crowd-funding platforms. A well-executed prototype showcases the potential of the game, making it easier to generate interest and secure funding or support. It provides a tangible demonstration of the game's unique selling points, gameplay mechanics, and overall experience, allowing potential stakeholders to experience first-hand the essence of the game and its potential market appeal.

In summary, prototyping is a vital aspect of game design that empowers designers to validate their concepts, gather feedback, refine mechanics, and mitigate risks. It fosters creativity, facilitates effective communication and collaboration, and supports an iterative design process. By leveraging the power of prototyping, game designers can create more compelling and successful games that captivate and delight players.

Creating rough gameplay mechanics and levels

When it comes to creating rough gameplay mechanics and levels, game designers embark on a creative journey to conceptualize and shape the core interactive elements of the game. This process involves several key steps and considerations to ensure a compelling and engaging player experience.

The first step is to establish the foundational gameplay mechanics. Game designers brainstorm and ideate various gameplay concepts, exploring mechanics that align with the game's genre, theme, and overall vision. They consider factors such as player interaction, character abilities, objectives, challenges, and progression systems. By defining these mechanics, designers lay the groundwork for the player's interactive experience within the game.

Once the core gameplay mechanics are defined, designers proceed to create rough prototypes or mock-ups. These prototypes can take various forms, from simple sketches or wireframes to digital prototypes using game development tools or specialized software. The purpose of these rough prototypes is to test and iterate on the mechanics, evaluating their effectiveness and identifying potential areas for improvement.

In parallel with refining the gameplay mechanics, game designers also start crafting rough level designs. Level design involves structuring the game's environments, challenges, and progression to create engaging and cohesive gameplay experiences. Designers consider factors such as the pacing of the game, the placement of obstacles and rewards, the balance of difficulty, and the overall flow of the player's journey.

During the creation of rough gameplay mechanics and levels, playtesting plays a crucial role. Game designers conduct internal play-tests or gather feedback from colleagues and testers to assess the effectiveness of their designs. Playtesting helps identify potential issues, such as imbalances in difficulty, unclear objectives, or unanticipated player behaviours. Feedback from playtesting sessions informs the iteration and refinement of the gameplay mechanics and level designs.

Throughout the process, game designers closely collaborate

with other members of the development team, such as artists, programmers, and level designers. This collaboration ensures that the gameplay mechanics and levels align with the overall vision of the game and complement other aspects, such as the visual style, audio design, and narrative elements.

As the rough gameplay mechanics and levels evolve and improve, designers document and communicate their designs through various means. This documentation helps provide clear guidelines and references for the development team, ensuring that everyone involved understands and implements the intended gameplay mechanics and level designs accurately.

In summary, creating rough gameplay mechanics and levels is a dynamic and iterative process that involves conceptualizing, prototyping, playtesting, and refining. It requires a combination of creativity, analytical thinking, and a deep understanding of player experience. By crafting compelling gameplay mechanics and well-designed levels, game designers lay the foundation for immersive and engaging player experiences in the final game.

System Mapping and Gameplay Mechanics

System mapping is a valuable technique used by game designers to visualize and analyze the interconnected systems and mechanics within a game. It involves creating a visual representation, often in the form of diagrams or flowcharts, that illustrates the relationships, dependencies, and interactions between different game elements.

The process of system mapping begins with identifying the core systems and mechanics that define the gameplay experience. This includes systems such as movement, combat, resource management, progression, and more. Game designers carefully analyze each system and its components to understand how they contribute to the overall gameplay dynamics.

Next, they map out the connections between these systems, depicting how they interact and influence one another. This can be done through visual representations, such as arrows or lines connecting different elements, indicating the flow of information, actions, or effects between them. For example, a system mapping diagram might illustrate how player actions in combat affect the health of enemies or how collecting resources impacts the player's inventory.

System mapping helps game designers gain a holistic view of the game's mechanics and how they work together as a cohesive whole. It allows them to identify potential issues, imbalances, or gaps in gameplay, enabling them to make informed design decisions and adjustments.

Through system mapping, game designers can also experiment with different variations or alternatives for specific systems. They can create multiple maps to explore different design possibilities and evaluate the potential impact on gameplay. This iterative approach helps them refine and optimize the systems to achieve the desired player experience.

Furthermore, system mapping is a valuable communication tool. It facilitates effective collaboration with other team members by providing a visual reference for discussing and understanding the intricate relationships between different game elements. Artists, programmers, and other stakeholders can easily grasp the overall structure and interactions of the game's systems, enabling them to align their work and contributions accordingly.

System mapping is a powerful technique that allows game designers to analyze, visualize, and refine the interconnected systems and mechanics of a game. It helps them create a well-balanced and engaging gameplay experience by providing a comprehensive understanding of how different elements work together. System mapping supports the iterative design process and effective collaboration, ensuring that the game's systems are thoughtfully designed and harmoniously integrated.

Gameplay Mechanics Documentation

Mechanics documentation is a process in game design that involves capturing and detailing the various gameplay mechanics and systems that will be present in the game. It serves as a comprehensive reference and guide for the development team, ensuring that everyone involved in the project has a clear understanding of how the game mechanics function and interact with each other.

The purpose of mechanics documentation is to provide a structured and organized overview of the game's mechanics, outlining their functionality, rules, and relationships. It helps ensure consistency, coherence, and balance in the gameplay experience.

To create mechanics documentation, game designers typically start by identifying the core mechanics that drive the gameplay. These can include movement, combat, puzzles, resource management, progression systems, and more. Each mechanic is then described in detail, specifying its purpose, rules, inputs, outputs, and any relevant dependencies or constraints.

The documentation may include diagrams, flowcharts, or visual representations to illustrate the flow and interactions between different mechanics. This visual aid can help the development team visualize the relationships and dependencies between mechanics and understand how they contribute to the overall game experience.

In addition to describing individual mechanics, the documentation also covers how these mechanics work together to create a cohesive and engaging gameplay experience. It explains how mechanics synergize, complement, or build upon each other to provide depth and variety to the gameplay.

Mechanics documentation also addresses potential edge cases, exceptions, and special scenarios that may arise during gameplay. It helps the development team anticipate and plan for different player actions or choices, ensuring that the mechanics can handle a variety of player interactions and remain robust and balanced.

Furthermore, mechanics documentation can include guidelines and best practices for implementing and fine-tuning the mechanics. This information assists programmers, artists, and other members of the development team in understanding the technical requirements and considerations related to implementing the mechanics effectively.

The documentation serves as a communication tool, allowing designers to effectively convey their ideas and intentions to the development team. It ensures that everyone involved in the game's production is aligned and working towards a shared understanding of the gameplay mechanics.

As the development progresses, mechanics documentation may evolve and be updated to reflect changes, improvements, or new additions to the game's mechanics. It is a living document that adapts to the iterative nature of game development.

In summary, mechanics documentation is a vital component of game design that outlines and describes the various gameplay mechanics and systems. It provides a comprehensive reference for the development team, ensuring consistency, clarity, and effective implementation of the game's mechanics. By documenting the mechanics, designers can maintain a cohesive vision and guide the team towards creating a rich and enjoyable gameplay experience.

Iterative Design

Iterative design is a crucial process in game design that involves continuously refining and improving the game through a cycle of testing, feedback, and iteration. It is an iterative approach where designers create, evaluate, and refine game elements based on player feedback and data analysis.

The goal of iterative design is to enhance the overall gameplay experience by addressing issues, improving mechanics, and optimizing various aspects of the game. It allows designers to iterate on their ideas, experiment with different solutions, and make informed decisions based on real-world testing.

The iterative design process typically involves the following steps:

Design and Implementation: The initial design of the game is created, including mechanics, levels, characters, and other elements. These design ideas are then implemented in a playable prototype or a build of the game.

Playtesting: The game prototype is tested by a group of players or a target audience. Playtesting can be done in-house or through external playtesting sessions. The players' feedback and observations are collected, focusing on their experiences, challenges, preferences, and suggestions.

Feedback and Analysis: The feedback gathered from playtesting is carefully analyzed by the design team. This involves identifying patterns, trends, and common issues reported by players. The team also looks for positive aspects of the game that can be emphasized or expanded upon.

Iteration: Based on the feedback and analysis, the design team makes informed decisions on what aspects of the game need improvement or adjustment. They revise the design, mechanics, levels, or other elements to address the identified issues and enhance the gameplay experience.

Testing and Validation: The revised version of the game is tested again to evaluate the impact of the changes. This process helps the design team validate the effectiveness of their iterations and gather additional feedback for further improvements.

Repeat: The cycle of playtesting, feedback analysis, iteration, and retesting continues throughout the development process. The design team keeps refining the game based on the results of each iteration, continually improving and polishing the gameplay experience.

Iterative design offers several benefits to game designers. It allows them to:

Identify and address gameplay issues: By continuously testing the game with real players, designers can uncover flaws, inconsistencies, or areas of confusion in the gameplay. This feedback-driven approach helps them identify and address issues early on, ensuring a smoother and more enjoyable experience for players.

Optimize game mechanics and balance: Through iterative design, designers can fine-tune game mechanics, balance challenges, and adjust difficulty levels based on player feedback. This process helps them create a more engaging and satisfying gameplay experience.

Validate design decisions: Iterative design provides designers with the opportunity to validate their design choices through player feedback. It helps them understand how players perceive and respond to various elements of the game, allowing for informed design decisions and adjustments.

Foster innovation and creativity: By embracing an iterative approach, designers can experiment with new ideas, take risks, and explore innovative concepts. They can test unconventional mechanics, gameplay structures, or narrative approaches, gaining insights and pushing the boundaries of game design.

Increase player engagement and retention: Through iterative design, designers can refine the game to enhance player engagement, improve pacing, and increase replay value. By addressing player preferences and expectations, they can create a game that captivates and retains the interest of the target audience.

In summary, iterative design is a vital process in game design that involves continuously refining and improving the game based on player feedback and analysis. It allows designers to address issues, optimize mechanics, validate design decisions, foster innovation, and create an engaging gameplay experience. By embracing an iterative approach, designers can evolve their game towards its fullest potential, resulting in a polished and immersive player experience.

Comparative Analysis

Comparative analysis is an important technique used by game designers to evaluate and understand the strengths and weaknesses of their own game in relation to other existing games in the market. It involves examining and comparing different aspects of games, such as mechanics, aesthetics, narrative, player experience, and overall design, to gain insights and inspiration for their own game.

The process of comparative analysis typically involves the following steps:

Identifying Reference Games: Game designers start by selecting a set of reference games that are relevant to their own game's genre, target audience, or design goals. These reference games can be both successful and influential titles or even lesser-known games that excel in specific aspects.

Analyzing Game Mechanics: The designers delve into the mechanics of the reference games to understand how they work, how different systems and elements interact, and how they contribute to the overall gameplay experience. This analysis helps identify innovative or effective mechanics that can be adapted or expanded upon in their own game.

Evaluating Player Experience: Comparative analysis involves examining the player experience in reference games, including elements such as pacing, difficulty, player agency, engagement, and satisfaction. Designers analyze how the games create immersion, evoke emotions, and deliver meaningful experiences to players.

Assessing Aesthetics and Presentation: The visual and audio aspects of reference games are examined to understand how they contribute to the overall atmosphere, storytelling, and player engagement. This analysis helps designers gain inspiration for creating captivating visuals, compelling sound design, and immersive environments in their own game.

Considering Narrative and Storytelling: If narrative is an important component of the game being designed, comparative analysis involves studying the storytelling techniques, character development, plot structures, and narrative arcs of reference games. This analysis helps designers identify effective narrative approaches and storytelling methods that resonate with players.

Extracting Lessons and Inspiration: Throughout the comparative analysis, designers extract valuable lessons, insights, and inspiration from the reference games. They identify successful design choices, innovative solutions, or unique features that can be adapted or applied to their own game. This process helps spark creativity and guide the development of their game's unique identity.

The benefits of comparative analysis for game designers are significant:

Insights into Best Practices: By analyzing successful games, designers can gain insights into best practices and industry standards. They can understand what works well in certain genres or player experiences and use that knowledge to inform their own design decisions.

Identification of Unique Selling Points: Comparative analysis helps designers identify the unique aspects or features that set their game apart from others in the market. By understanding what makes other games successful, they can refine and emphasize the aspects that make their game stand out.

Inspiration for Innovation: By examining different games and their design approaches, designers can find inspiration for innovative ideas and novel solutions. They can adapt and combine existing concepts to create new and exciting gameplay experiences.

Avoiding Design Pitfalls: Analyzing the weaknesses or limitations of other games can help designers avoid common pitfalls or design flaws. They can learn from the mistakes of others and make informed choices to create a more polished and well-rounded game.

Understanding Player Expectations: Comparative analysis provides valuable insights into player preferences and expectations. By studying popular games, designers can understand what players enjoy and what aspects contribute to a satisfying gaming experience. This understanding allows them to align their own game's design with player expectations.

In summary, comparative analysis is a valuable technique used by game designers to evaluate and gain insights from existing games. It helps them understand game mechanics, evaluate player experience, explore aesthetics and presentation, consider narrative approaches, and extract valuable lessons and inspiration. By leveraging the strengths of successful games and learning from their weaknesses, designers can create unique, engaging, and well-crafted games that resonate with their target audience.

Testing and refining the prototype based on player feedback

Testing and refining the prototype game based on player feedback is a crucial step in the game design process. It allows game designers to gather insights, identify strengths and weaknesses, and make informed improvements to enhance the overall player experience. Here's a breakdown of how game designers test and refine the prototype game:

Plan and conduct playtesting: Game designers carefully plan playtesting sessions, inviting a diverse group of players who represent the game's target audience. They provide clear instructions and objectives for the playtesters to follow. During the playtesting session, designers observe players' actions, reactions, and feedback while taking notes.

Collect qualitative and quantitative feedback: Designers collect both qualitative and quantitative feedback from the playtesters. Qualitative feedback involves open-ended questions, interviews, or group discussions to gather players' thoughts, opinions, and suggestions. Quantitative feedback includes data such as completion times, success rates, or player ratings that provide measurable insights.

Analyze feedback: Game designers thoroughly analyze the collected feedback, looking for patterns, common themes, and recurring issues. They prioritize the feedback based on its significance and relevance to the game's vision and goals. This analysis helps identify specific areas that require refinement or improvement.

Iterate and make improvements: Using the feedback as a guide, game designers iterate on the prototype, making targeted improvements and adjustments. They address the identified issues, refine the mechanics, tweak the level design, or enhance the overall gameplay experience. The goal is to address player concerns and create a more polished and engaging prototype.

Re-test and repeat: After implementing the improvements, designers conduct further playtesting sessions to evaluate the effectiveness of the changes. They observe how the revisions have impacted player experience and gather additional feedback. This iterative process of testing, refining, and re-testing continues until the prototype reaches a satisfactory level of quality and aligns with the intended player experience.

Document changes: Throughout the testing and refinement process, game designers document the changes made to the prototype. This documentation helps keep track of the iterative design decisions, ensuring consistency and providing a reference for future development stages.

By actively involving players in the testing process and incorporating their feedback, game designers can identify and address design flaws, improve game mechanics, enhance the overall gameplay experience, and align the prototype with the intended vision. This iterative and player-centric approach ensures that the final game resonates with the target audience and delivers an engaging and satisfying experience.

Balancing gameplay elements and difficulty

Balancing gameplay elements and difficulty is a critical aspect of game design that requires careful consideration and iteration. Game designers aim to create a challenging yet enjoyable experience that keeps players engaged without becoming frustrating or too easy. Here are some key considerations and strategies that game designers employ to achieve this balance:

Define the target audience: Understanding the target audience is crucial for determining the appropriate difficulty level. Different types of players have varying skill levels, preferences, and expectations. Game designers must identify the intended audience and tailor the gameplay experience accordingly.

Gradual learning curve: Designers often implement a gradual learning curve to introduce gameplay mechanics and challenges in a progressive manner. They start with simpler tasks to familiarize players with the game mechanics and gradually increase the difficulty as players become more proficient. This allows players to build their skills and confidence gradually, preventing overwhelming experiences.

Player feedback and playtesting: Playtesting with a diverse group of players helps gather feedback on the game's difficulty. Designers observe player behavior, analyze their performance, and collect feedback to identify areas that may be too challenging or too easy. This feedback is valuable for making informed adjustments and fine-tuning the difficulty to strike the right balance.

Adjustable difficulty options: Providing adjustable difficulty options allows players to customize their gameplay experience based on their skill level and preferences. Game designers may include multiple difficulty modes, such as easy, normal, and hard, or provide sliders or settings that allow players to modify specific aspects of the game's challenge, such as enemy strength or puzzle complexity.

Iterative design and balancing: Balancing gameplay elements and difficulty is an iterative process. Game designers continually test and refine the game to ensure that the challenge remains engaging and fair. They make adjustments to enemy AI, level design, puzzles, or combat mechanics based on player feedback and observation. By carefully analyzing player behaviour and performance, designers can identify potential areas of imbalance and make necessary adjustments.

Progressive rewards and pacing: Balancing gameplay elements also involves considering the pacing and reward structure. Designers strategically place rewards, such as power-ups or new abilities, throughout the game to motivate and reward players for overcoming challenges. Balancing the frequency and impact of these rewards contributes to the overall sense of progression and keeps players motivated to continue playing.

Accessible design: Game designers also aim to make their games accessible to a wide range of players. They consider factors such as clear instructions, intuitive controls, and well-designed user interfaces that contribute to a smoother gameplay experience. Removing unnecessary frustrations and barriers allows players to focus on the core challenges and enjoy the game.

Achieving a balance between gameplay elements and difficulty requires a combination of design intuition, player feedback, and iterative refinement. Game designers must consider the skill level and preferences of their target audience, provide gradual challenges, and adjust the difficulty based on testing and feedback. By carefully fine-tuning the gameplay experience, designers can create a game that offers an enjoyable and rewarding challenge for players.

Chapter 5 - Production: Bringing the Vision to Life

In the production phase of game design, the games designer plays a crucial role in bringing the creative vision to life. Collaborating closely with artists, programmers, sound designers, and other team members, the designer ensures that the game's mechanics, aesthetics, and narrative elements are seamlessly integrated. They provide guidance and support throughout the development process, overseeing the implementation of gameplay systems, level designs, and visual assets. With meticulous attention to detail and a strong understanding of player experience, the games designer ensures that the final product aligns with the original vision while meeting technical constraints and project timelines. By overseeing the production phase, the games designer plays a key role in transforming ideas and concepts into a fully realized and immersive gaming experience.

Building the game's framework and architecture

Building the game's framework and architecture is a critical aspect of game design that lays the foundation for a cohesive and scalable game development process. The games designer is responsible for designing and implementing the underlying structure and systems that will support the game's mechanics, features, and content. This involves creating an organized framework that allows for efficient development, easy maintenance, and flexibility for future iterations.

To begin, the games designer starts by defining the overall structure of the game. This includes determining the game's core systems, such as the input and control system, physics engine, AI system, and rendering pipeline. By carefully planning and architecting these systems, the designer ensures that they work together harmoniously, providing a solid backbone for the game.

Once the core systems are in place, the games designer moves on to designing the game's framework. This involves creating a set of rules, conventions, and guidelines that govern how various game components interact with each other. For example, the designer might establish guidelines for how different game objects can communicate, how data is stored and accessed, and how events and actions are triggered. By establishing a clear framework, the designer facilitates a consistent and coherent development process.

Another important aspect of building the game's framework is designing the game's entity-component system. This architectural pattern allows for flexible and modular game development by separating the game's entities (such as characters, objects, or enemies) into individual components that can be added, removed, or modified independently. The games designer determines the components needed for the game, defines their behavior and interactions, and establishes the rules for how they can be combined to create complex gameplay elements.

In addition to the framework, the games designer is also responsible for designing the game's architecture. This involves structuring the game's codebase in a way that promotes readability, maintainability, and scalability. The designer may employ design patterns and software engineering principles to create a well-organized and extensible codebase. By structuring the code effectively, the designer enables other team members, such as programmers and artists, to work collaboratively and efficiently.

Throughout the process of building the game's framework and architecture, the games designer must consider the project's scope, technical constraints, and performance requirements. They must strike a balance between flexibility and efficiency, ensuring that the framework can accommodate the game's intended features while maintaining optimal performance.

Ultimately, building the game's framework and architecture is a complex and iterative process that requires careful planning, design, and implementation. The games designer's expertise in creating a solid foundation paves the way for a smooth and successful game development journey, enabling the team to build upon the framework and bring the game's vision to life.

Collaborating with programmers and artists to implement assets

When it comes to implementing assets in a game, collaboration between game designers, programmers and artists is absolutely vital. They work closely together to ensure that the assets are seamlessly integrated into the game and perfectly align with the overall vision and design.

When collaborating with programmers, game designers provide detailed documentation and guidelines that outline the functionality and behaviour expected from the assets. This includes specifying how the assets should interact with the game world, characters, and other elements. Through regular communication and feedback exchanges, the designer and programmer address technical challenges and design iterations during the implementation process. Together, they determine the technical requirements and constraints, such as file formats, performance optimization, and integration with game systems.

In addition, game designers collaborate with artists to ensure that the visual assets harmonize with the intended artistic direction and design aesthetics. By providing art direction, reference materials, and style guides, the designer guides the artists in creating assets that seamlessly fit within the game's visual style. This collaboration involves an iterative process of feedback and refinement to achieve the desired visual quality and consistency. The designer offers feedback on concept art, character designs, environment assets, and other visual elements to maintain alignment and achieve the desired outcome.

Throughout the collaboration, effective communication and clear documentation play a crucial role. Game designers need to effectively convey their design intentions and requirements to both programmers and artists, ensuring that everyone shares a common understanding of the desired outcomes. Visual aids, written explanations, and interactive prototypes are utilized to articulate design ideas and demonstrate how the assets should function and appear in the game. Regular meetings, reviews, and feedback sessions are held to foster alignment and address any issues or discrepancies that may arise.

Furthermore, collaboration often extends beyond the initial implementation phase. As the game evolves and new features or adjustments are made, game designers continue to work closely with programmers and artists to iterate on existing assets or create new ones. This ongoing collaborative process allows for continuous improvement and refinement, ensuring that the final game incorporates the best possible assets to enhance the player experience.

In summary, collaboration between game designers, programmers, and artists is pivotal for the successful implementation of assets in a game. Through effective communication, clear documentation, and regular feedback exchanges, they ensure that the assets meet technical requirements, align with the design vision, and contribute to a cohesive and immersive player experience. This collaborative environment enables the merging of ideas and skills, ultimately bringing the game to life in the best possible way.

Here's an example of a collaboration between a game designer and an artist to prepare assets for a game:

Let's say the game designer is working on a fantasy RPG and needs character designs for the game's main protagonist. They discuss the vision for the character with the artist, providing details about the character's personality, backstory, and role within the game's narrative.

The game designer and artist have several meetings to exchange ideas and references. The designer shares concept art, mood boards, and visual inspirations to help the artist understand the desired aesthetics and style. They discuss the character's appearance, including their outfit, weapons, and unique features.

Based on these discussions, the artist creates a series of rough sketches, presenting different design options for the protagonist. The game designer reviews the sketches and provides feedback, suggesting changes or enhancements to align the designs more closely with the game's vision.

Once the rough sketches are refined and approved, the artist proceeds to create more detailed concept art. They focus on capturing the character's personality, expressions, and overall look. The game designer collaborates closely with the artist during this stage, providing feedback and guidance to ensure that the concept art accurately represents the intended character.

After the concept art is finalized, the artist starts working on the final character assets, such as the high-resolution character model, textures, and animations. The game designer regularly checks in with the artist to review the progress, ensuring that the assets are aligned with the approved concept art and that any necessary adjustments are made.

Once the character assets are completed, the game designer works with the programming team to integrate them into the game. They provide the necessary specifications and instructions to ensure the character moves and behaves as intended, considering factors like combat animations, interactions with the environment, and dialogue sequences.

Throughout the collaboration, the game designer and artist maintain open communication, exchanging ideas and addressing any challenges or revisions that arise. They work together to ensure that the character assets are not only visually appealing but also enhance the player's immersion and connection with the game's world.

This example illustrates how a game designer and an artist collaborate to create and implement character assets for a game. Their close collaboration, regular feedback exchanges, and shared understanding of the game's vision contribute to the successful integration of visually captivating and thematically appropriate assets into the final game.

Here's an example of a collaboration between a game designer and a programmer to prepare assets for a game:

Let's imagine the game designer is working on a platformer game and needs to implement a new gameplay mechanic involving a grappling hook. They discuss the concept and functionality of the grappling hook with the programmer, providing details on how it should behave, its range, and the player's interaction with it.

The game designer and programmer have multiple discussions to exchange ideas and clarify the technical requirements. They brainstorm together to determine the best approach for implementing the grappling hook mechanic within the game's existing framework. The designer emphasizes the importance of smooth and responsive controls, as well as the desired visual effects and audio cues to enhance the player's experience.

Based on these discussions, the programmer starts working on implementing the grappling hook mechanic. They write the necessary code to create the functionality, considering factors such as the physics simulation, collision detection, and player input. The programmer ensures that the grappling hook integrates seamlessly with the player's movement and other game mechanics.

During the implementation process, the game designer regularly collaborates with the programmer to provide feedback and make adjustments. They playtest the mechanic together, evaluating its feel and effectiveness. The designer shares their observations and suggests tweaks to improve the mechanic's responsiveness, balance, or visual presentation.

Once the grappling hook mechanic is implemented and refined, the game designer and programmer collaborate further to integrate corresponding visual and audio assets. The designer provides art assets for the grappling hook, such as its appearance, animations, and particle effects, while also specifying the desired sound effects and accompanying audio cues.

The programmer integrates the visual and audio assets into the game, ensuring that they synchronize with the gameplay mechanics. They fine-tune parameters and timings to enhance the overall experience. The game designer and programmer work closely together to address any issues or discrepancies, aiming for a seamless integration of assets and functionality.

Throughout the collaboration, the game designer and programmer maintain open communication and iterate on the implementation as needed. They troubleshoot together, test different scenarios, and refine the mechanic until it meets the intended design goals.

This example demonstrates how a game designer and a programmer collaborate to implement gameplay assets, specifically focusing on a grappling hook mechanic. Their collaboration involves extensive discussions, iterative development, and continuous feedback exchanges to ensure the successful integration of the mechanic into the game, resulting in an engaging and polished gameplay experience.

Iterating and refining gameplay mechanics and features

During the production of a video game, game designers employ iterative processes to continuously iterate and refine gameplay mechanics and features.

Here's a detailed explanation of how they go about it:

Playtesting and Evaluation: Game designers organize playtesting sessions to gather feedback from players. They observe how players interact with the game, analyze their experiences, and identify areas that need improvement. This feedback serves as a valuable resource for identifying gameplay mechanics and features that require iteration and refinement.

Analyzing Player Data: Game designers utilize player data collected during playtesting and gameplay sessions. They examine metrics such as player progression, completion rates, engagement levels, and any recorded issues or bugs. This data provides insights into specific areas where gameplay mechanics and features can be refined to enhance the player experience.

Iterative Design Process: Based on the feedback and data analysis, game designers engage in an iterative design process. They make incremental changes and updates to gameplay mechanics and features, focusing on addressing identified issues, enhancing player enjoyment, and improving the overall balance of the game.

Prototyping and Mock-ups: To test and experiment with potential improvements, game designers create prototypes or mock-ups. These serve as a platform for implementing and iterating upon refined gameplay mechanics and features. Prototypes allow designers to quickly assess the impact of their changes and gather additional feedback from playtesting sessions.

Collaboration with Development Team: Game designers collaborate closely with the development team, including programmers, artists, and other stakeholders. They communicate their design changes and refinements, providing clear documentation and guidelines. Collaboration ensures that the implementation of the refined gameplay mechanics and features aligns with the designer's vision.

Balancing and Fine-Tuning: Balancing gameplay mechanics and features is a crucial aspect of iteration. Game designers fine-tune elements such as difficulty, progression, pacing, rewards, and challenges to create a cohesive and engaging experience. They carefully consider player feedback, data analysis, and their own expertise to strike the right balance that provides both enjoyment and a sense of challenge.

Testing and Validation: As the refined gameplay mechanics and features are implemented, game designers conduct extensive testing to validate the changes. They assess how the refinements integrate with other aspects of the game, ensure they function as intended, and evaluate their impact on the overall player experience.

Continuous Improvement: The process of iterating and refining gameplay mechanics and features is ongoing throughout the production phase. Game designers continually gather feedback, make adjustments, and refine the game's mechanics and features to ensure they align with the desired player experience and meet the overall design goals.

By following these iterative processes and gathering feedback at various stages of production, game designers can refine and improve gameplay mechanics and features. This iterative approach ensures that the game evolves and optimizes the player experience as it progresses towards completion.

Managing timelines, milestones, and resource

allocation

During the production of a video game, game designers play a crucial role in managing timelines, milestones, and resource allocation. They employ several strategies and techniques to ensure the smooth progress of the project.

Here's an alternative explanation of how game designers handle these responsibilities:

To begin, game designers collaborate with project managers and stakeholders to define the scope and objectives of the project. This sets the stage for effective project management. Together, they create a detailed production plan that includes a development timeline, major milestones, and deadlines for key deliverables.

Resource allocation is a significant aspect of the game designer's role. They carefully assess the resources required for each phase of production, such as personnel, tools, technology, and assets. Working closely with project managers, they assign resources based on availability and skills, and strive for a balanced distribution of workload.

Many game designers adopt agile development methodologies, like Scrum or Kanban, to manage timelines and milestones effectively. They break the development process into smaller iterations called sprints, each with defined goals, timelines, and deliverables. This approach allows for flexibility and adaptation as the project progresses.

Tracking progress and milestones is essential for game designers. They use project management tools and techniques, such as Gantt charts or task management software, to monitor tasks, dependencies, and resource allocation. Regular team meetings and status updates keep everyone informed about progress and any potential issues or delays.

Risk management is another critical aspect of timeline and milestone management. Game designers pro-actively identify and address potential risks that may impact the project schedule. They develop contingency plans and collaborate with the team to mitigate risks and ensure smooth progress.

Communication and collaboration are vital throughout the production process. Game designers work closely with the development team, stakeholders, and external partners to ensure everyone is aligned on project timelines and objectives. They conduct regular meetings, provide updates, and address any concerns that may affect the production schedule.

As the game evolves, game designers make iterative adjustments to timelines, milestones, and resource allocation. They prioritize tasks based on changing requirements, feedback, and unforeseen circumstances. This agile approach allows for adaptability and optimization of the production process.

Quality assurance and testing receive dedicated attention from game designers. They allocate sufficient time and resources to ensure proper testing procedures are in place. This iterative testing process helps identify and address bugs, usability issues, and gameplay imbalances, ensuring a high-quality final product.

Continual evaluation and adjustment are integral to effective timeline and milestone management. Game designers regularly assess project progress and resource allocation to identify areas for improvement. They learn from challenges encountered, refine their management strategies, and apply those insights to future projects.

By effectively managing timelines, milestones, and resource allocation, game designers contribute to the successful delivery of a high-quality game within the established time frame. Their ability to balance these factors ensures the

production process remains on track and resources are
utilized efficiently.

Chapter 6 - Art and Audio Design

Art and audio design are the magical tools that empower games designers to craft truly remarkable and unforgettable gaming experiences. Through intricate visuals and captivating soundscapes, art and audio design breathe life into virtual worlds, shaping the atmosphere, emotions, and overall player engagement. The artistry of a games designer lies in their ability to use visuals to create stunning environments, mesmerizing characters, and breathtaking details that immerse players in a rich and immersive narrative.

Meanwhile, audio design enhances the gameplay by complementing the visual elements, setting the mood, and evoking emotions through captivating music, realistic sound effects, and immersive audio landscapes. By seamlessly integrating art and audio design, the games designer orchestrates a symphony of sights and sounds that elevates the player's experience to unprecedented levels of wonder and excitement.

Crafting visually appealing and immersive game worlds

Game designers play a crucial role in the art and audio design of a game, collaborating with artists and sound designers to create a cohesive and immersive experience. Here's how game designers contribute to the art and audio design:

Artistic Direction: Game designers work closely with artists to establish the artistic direction of the game. They provide creative input and guidance on the visual style, aesthetics, and thematic elements that align with the game's vision and intended player experience. This collaboration ensures that the art direction supports the game's narrative, gameplay mechanics, and overall design goals.

Conceptualization and Visualization: Game designers actively participate in the conceptualization and visualization process. They work with artists to translate ideas, themes, and gameplay mechanics into visual elements such as character designs, environments, objects, and user interfaces. Through discussions, sketches, storyboards, and mock-ups, game designers help shape the visual representation of the game world.

Asset Integration and Placement: Game designers are responsible for integrating art assets into the game engine and placing them within the game world. They work closely with artists to ensure that assets are properly implemented, optimized, and aligned with the gameplay requirements. Game designers consider factors such as visual hierarchy, level design, and player navigation to strategically place art assets and create a visually appealing and coherent experience.

Audio Integration and Gameplay Enhancement: Game designers collaborate with sound designers and composers to integrate audio elements into the game. They work together to determine the appropriate sound effects, music, and voiceovers that enhance gameplay, immerse players in the game world, and evoke the desired emotional responses. Game designers consider the timing, intensity, and spatial aspects of audio to create an engaging and immersive audio experience.

Narrative and Emotional Impact: Game designers collaborate with artists and sound designers to ensure that the visual and audio elements align with the game's narrative and desired emotional impact. They work together to convey storytelling elements, atmosphere, and character traits through visuals and sound. This collaboration enhances the player's emotional engagement, strengthens the game's themes, and creates a memorable experience.

User Interface and User Experience (UI/UX): Game

designers play a significant role in the UI/UX design process, collaborating with artists and UI/UX designers to create intuitive and visually appealing user interfaces. They provide input on the layout, visual style, iconography, and usability aspects of the UI, ensuring it aligns with the game's aesthetics and enhances the overall user experience.

Iterative Feedback and Refinement: Throughout the development process, game designers provide feedback and collaborate with artists and sound designers to refine the art and audio design. They review and iterate on visual and audio assets, provide suggestions for improvements, and ensure that the final implementation meets the intended vision and quality standards.

A games designer plays a pivotal role in shaping the audio and art design of a game, working closely with artists and sound designers to create a visually stunning and sonically immersive experience. They contribute to the artistic direction by providing creative input and guidance on the visual style, aesthetics, and thematic elements that align with the game's vision and intended player experience. Together with the artists, they participate in the conceptualization and visualization process, translating ideas and gameplay mechanics into captivating visual elements such as character designs, environments, objects, and user interfaces.

The games designer is responsible for integrating the art assets into the game engine and strategically placing them within the game world. They consider factors like visual hierarchy, level design, and player navigation to ensure that the art assets are implemented optimally and create a visually appealing and coherent experience. Additionally, they collaborate with sound designers and composers to integrate audio elements that enhance gameplay and immerse players in the game world. Together, they determine the appropriate sound effects, music, and voiceovers that evoke the desired emotional responses and enrich the overall audio experience.

The games designer ensures that the visual and audio elements align with the game's narrative and desired emotional impact. They work in collaboration with the artists and sound designers to convey storytelling elements, atmosphere, and character traits through visuals and sound. By integrating the narrative themes and emotional tones into the art and audio design, they enhance the player's emotional engagement, strengthen the game's themes, and create a memorable experience.

Moreover, the games designer actively participates in the UI/UX design process, collaborating with artists and UI/UX designers to create user-friendly and visually appealing interfaces. They provide input on the layout, visual style, iconography, and usability aspects of the user interface, ensuring that it aligns with the game's aesthetics and enhances the overall user experience.

Throughout the development process, the games designer provides iterative feedback and collaborates with the artists and sound designers to refine the art and audio design. They review and iterate on visual and audio assets, providing suggestions for improvements and ensuring that the final implementation meets the intended vision and quality standards.

In summary, the games designer's involvement in shaping the audio and art design of a game is integral. Through collaboration with artists and sound designers, they bring their creative vision and understanding of gameplay to the design process, resulting in a visually stunning, sonically immersive, and cohesive experience that enhances the overall quality and impact of the game.

Creating character designs, environments, and animations

A game designer plays a crucial role in creating character designs, environments, and animations that bring a game to life. They work closely with artists, animators, and other team members to shape the visual aspects of the game.

Here's how a game designer contributes to each element:

Character Designs: Game designers collaborate with concept artists and character artists to develop the visual appearance and traits of the game's characters. They provide guidance on the character's personality, backstory, abilities, and overall role within the game. The designer ensures that the character designs align with the game's art style, narrative, and gameplay mechanics.

Environments: Game designers work with level designers and environmental artists to craft immersive and engaging game worlds. They define the visual direction, set the mood and atmosphere, and establish the overall aesthetic of the environments. The designer considers factors like the game's genre, target audience, and gameplay requirements to create environments that enhance the player's experience and support the game's narrative.

Animations: Game designers collaborate with animators to create animations that bring characters, objects, and the game world to life. They provide input on the specific movements, actions, and behaviours required for gameplay and storytelling. The designer ensures that the animations are smooth, responsive, and visually appealing, contributing to the overall immersion and player engagement.

In all these aspects, the game designer serves as a bridge between the artistic vision and the gameplay mechanics. They ensure that the visual elements align with the game's design goals, enhance the player's experience, and effectively communicate the game's themes and narratives. Collaboration, effective communication, and a deep understanding of the game's vision are key to successfully creating captivating character designs, environments, and animations.

Example of a games designer working with a character artist in order to create a character for a video game:

Meet Sarah, a talented game designer, and Alex, an experienced character artist. They are collaborating on a new video game project called "Mystic Quest." Sarah's vision for the game involves a mystical world filled with unique and diverse characters.

Sarah begins by discussing her concept with Alex, sharing details about the game's setting, narrative, and gameplay mechanics. They brainstorm together, exploring various character ideas and narrowing down the key attributes they want to emphasize.

Based on their discussions, Sarah creates a design brief that outlines the character's personality, appearance, and role within the game. She describes a protagonist named Maya, a young sorceress with a strong connection to nature and magical abilities.

Sarah provides Alex with reference materials, such as mood boards, sketches, and written descriptions, to help visualize Maya. They discuss elements like Maya's clothing, hairstyle, facial features, and distinguishing accessories. Sarah emphasizes the importance of capturing Maya's magical aura and a sense of adventure in her design.

Alex takes the information and begins sketching initial concepts for Maya. They iterate on the designs, sharing feedback and making adjustments to ensure the character aligns with Sarah's vision. Once they agree on a concept, Alex creates detailed illustrations and renders, showcasing Maya's appearance from different angles and in various poses.

Throughout the process, Sarah offers input and provides guidance on how Maya's design can enhance the game's narrative and gameplay. They consider factors like readability, animation potential, and visual appeal to ensure Maya resonates with players.

As the collaboration progresses, Sarah and Alex continually communicate and iterate on the character design. They discuss the implementation of Maya's abilities, animations, and interactions within the game world. Sarah considers how Maya's design can convey her personality and progress visually as players advance through the game.

In the end, Sarah and Alex successfully bring Maya to life, creating a visually captivating and memorable character that embodies the essence of "Mystic Quest." The collaboration between the game designer and the character artist showcases the importance of effective communication, shared vision, and iterative design in the creation of compelling game characters.

Example of a games designer working with level designers and environmental artists to craft immersive and engaging game world:

Imagine a game designer named Mike working closely with level designers and environmental artists to create an immersive and engaging game world for their new project, "Lost Kingdom."

Mike starts by conceptualizing the game's world, envisioning a vast and mysterious ancient kingdom filled with lush forests, towering mountains, and hidden ruins. He communicates his ideas to the level designers and environmental artists, emphasizing the importance of creating an immersive and visually captivating experience for players.

Together, they collaborate to develop a cohesive vision for the game world. Mike shares reference materials, such as concept art, mood boards, and written descriptions, to guide the level designers and environmental artists in capturing the desired atmosphere and aesthetics.

The level designers begin by creating rough layouts and sketches of the game's environments, focusing on key locations like the dense forest, a majestic castle, and a treacherous mountain range. Mike reviews these designs, providing feedback on the placement of obstacles, points of interest, and overall flow of the gameplay.

Once the level designs are approved, the environmental artists step in to bring the world to life. They meticulously craft the details of each location, adding foliage, rocks, water bodies, and architectural elements that align with the game's theme. Mike and the environmental artists collaborate closely, discussing lighting, color palettes, and mood to enhance the atmosphere and evoke the desired emotions from players.

During the process, the level designers and environmental artists work in tandem, refining and iterating on their respective elements. They ensure a seamless integration between the gameplay and the visual aesthetics of the game world, striving to create a sense of immersion and exploration.

Mike conducts playtests and gathers feedback from testers, evaluating how the game world impacts the player experience. He collaborates with the level designers and environmental artists to make necessary adjustments and improvements based on the feedback, refining the game world to optimize player engagement.

Through their collective efforts, Mike, the level designers, and the environmental artists succeed in crafting an immersive and engaging game world for "Lost Kingdom." The collaboration between the game designer, level designers, and environmental artists highlights the importance of effective communication, shared vision, and iterative design in creating game worlds that captivate and transport players to new and exciting experiences.

Designing and integrating sound effects and music

A game designer plays a crucial role in the creation, design, and integration of sound effects and music to enhance the overall gaming experience.

Here's a breakdown of how a game designer contributes to this aspect of game development:

Sound Design Conceptualization: The game designer collaborates with sound designers and composers to define the desired audio atmosphere and style for the game. They discuss the game's theme, setting, and narrative to establish a cohesive vision for the sound design.

Sound Effects: The game designer works closely with sound designers to identify key moments, actions, and events in the game that require sound effects. They provide detailed briefs, references, and specifications to guide the creation of custom sound effects or the selection of pre-existing ones from sound libraries. The game designer ensures that the sound effects align with the gameplay mechanics, animations, and player interactions, enhancing immersion and reinforcing the game's audio-visual feedback loop.

Music Composition: The game designer collaborates with composers to create original music that complements the game's mood, pacing, and narrative. They communicate the desired emotions, themes, and musical styles to guide the composition process. The game designer may also provide specific cues or musical transitions for different gameplay situations, such as intense action sequences, exploration, or emotional moments.

Audio Integration: The game designer is responsible for integrating sound effects and music into the game engine. They work closely with programmers to ensure seamless playback and synchronization of audio assets. This includes implementing audio triggers, spatialization, and dynamic audio systems that respond to in-game events and player actions. The game designer meticulously tests and adjusts the audio mix to achieve a balanced and immersive audio experience.

Iterative Feedback and Polishing: Throughout the development process, the game designer continuously reviews and provides feedback on the sound effects and music. They evaluate how the audio enhances or detracts from the gameplay, ensuring that it aligns with the intended player experience. The game designer collaborates with the sound team to make necessary adjustments, polish the audio assets, and optimize performance.

Playtesting and Player Feedback: The game designer conducts playtests to gather feedback from players regarding the audio experience. They analyze how the sound effects and music impact player engagement, emotion, and immersion. Based on the feedback, the game designer iterates on the audio design, making refinements to enhance the overall quality and impact of the sound and music.

By actively participating in the creation, design, and integration of sound effects and music, the game designer contributes to crafting a cohesive and immersive audio experience that complements the gameplay, heightens emotions, and brings the game world to life.

Here's an example of a game designer working with sound designers to design and integrate sound effects and music into a game:

Game Designer (GD): Hey, we're working on a futuristic sci-fi game, and we need to create a captivating audio experience to immerse players in this high-tech world. Let's collaborate on the sound design and music. We'll need a mix of futuristic and atmospheric sounds, intense action cues, and ambient music to set the mood.

Sound Designer (SD): Absolutely! I'll start by creating a range of sound effects for various in-game actions, such as footsteps, weapon firing, and interactive objects. We can blend organic and synthesized sounds to achieve a futuristic vibe. I'll also design soundscapes for different environments, like bustling cityscapes, futuristic laboratories, and alien landscapes. We'll want to use spatial audio techniques to enhance the sense of depth and immersion.

GD: That sounds great! For the music, we'll need dynamic tracks that adapt to gameplay situations. Let's have a mix of ambient tracks for exploration and low-intensity moments, and more energetic music for combat or suspenseful sequences. We can work with composers to create tracks that seamlessly transition between different layers and intensities based on the player's actions.

SD: I'll collaborate with the composers to ensure the music aligns with the game's overall aesthetic and matches the desired emotional tone for each gameplay situation. We can experiment with different instrumentations, synthesizers, and electronic elements to achieve that futuristic sound you're looking for.

GD: Excellent! As we progress, we'll need to integrate the sound effects and music into the game engine. We want the audio to be dynamic and responsive, reacting to player actions and events. We should discuss implementing audio triggers that synchronize with in-game events, such as enemy encounters, puzzle completions, or cinematic moments.

SD: Definitely. I'll work closely with the programmers to set up these audio triggers and ensure that the sound effects and music seamlessly blend with the gameplay. We'll also explore techniques like adaptive audio, where the music intensifies or changes based on the player's performance or the game's narrative progression.

GD: Throughout development, we'll conduct playtests to gather feedback on the audio experience. We'll evaluate how well the sound effects and music enhance immersion, create tension, and evoke the desired emotions. Based on player feedback, we'll fine-tune the audio design, making adjustments to volume levels, spatialization, and timing for optimal impact.

SD: Sounds like a plan! I'll also ensure that the audio assets are optimized for performance and work within the technical constraints of the target platforms. We'll collaborate closely to refine and polish the sound effects and music, ensuring they enhance the overall gameplay experience and leave a lasting impression on players.

By working collaboratively, the game designer and sound designer can create a synergistic audio experience that elevates the game's atmosphere, enhances immersion, and amplifies the emotional impact for players.

Here's another example of a game designer working with a music composer to integrate music into a game and create an immersive atmosphere:

Game Designer (GD): Hey there! We're working on an awesome open-world fantasy RPG, and we need your help to make the music an integral part of the game's enchanting atmosphere. Let's team up to design and integrate some incredible sound effects and music that will transport players into the magical world we're creating.

Music Composer (MC): Absolutely! I'm thrilled to be a part of this adventure. Let's start by diving deep into the game's story and setting. Tell me all about the characters, locations, and the emotions we want to evoke. I'll craft melodies and themes that capture the essence of the game and make it come alive.

GD: That's fantastic! We have different regions in the game, each with its own unique flavour. We'll need music that reflects the diverse cultures and landscapes players will encounter. By infusing the music with the essence of each region, we can transport players to these magical places and make their journey truly immersive.

MC: I love the idea! I'll explore various musical styles and instruments that will resonate with each region. By creating melodies and arrangements that capture the spirit of these cultures, we'll add depth and authenticity to the game world. I'll also ensure that the music seamlessly adapts to the player's actions, enhancing their exploration and creating memorable moments.

GD: Perfect! We also have epic battles, emotional cutscenes, and moments of discovery. We need music that amplifies these experiences, getting players' hearts racing or tugging at their heartstrings. We want the music to be a powerful companion to the gameplay.

MC: Absolutely! I'll compose tracks that heighten the

excitement during battles, emphasize the emotional impact of key moments, and add a sense of wonder to exploration. We'll work together to ensure that the music aligns perfectly with the gameplay, syncing up with the action and drawing players further into the game's narrative.

GD: Throughout development, we'll have playtesting sessions where we gather feedback from players. We want to make sure the music hits all the right notes and enhances the overall player experience. Your input and creativity are invaluable in making the game truly immersive.

MC: I'm all for it! Collaboration is key, and I'll eagerly listen to player feedback to refine the compositions. We'll make sure the music integrates seamlessly with the game's audio systems, adding that extra layer of magic that keeps players hooked.

GD: Amazing! Your music will be the soundtrack of our players' adventures, and I can't wait to see and hear how it elevates the overall experience. Your talent and dedication will make this game truly special.

By collaborating closely with the music composer, the game designer ensures that the music becomes an integral part of the game's atmosphere, captivating players and immersing them in a world of wonder. Together, they bring the game to life with melodies, themes, and sound effects that enhance the gameplay, evoke emotions, and leave players with a truly memorable experience.

The role of art and audio in enhancing the player experience

Art and audio play crucial roles in enhancing the player experience in a video game, creating a rich and immersive world that captivates players. The visual elements, including character designs, environments, animations, and effects, are meticulously crafted to transport players into a visually stunning and believable game world. Detailed and well-designed environments, whether they are fantastical realms or realistic settings, contribute to the overall atmosphere and mood of the game. The art style, color palette, lighting, and visual effects work together to establish the desired tone, whether it's a bright and colorful world, a dark and ominous one, or anything in between. These visual elements not only serve as eye candy but also play a practical role in providing important gameplay information, such as indicating the health of characters, highlighting interactive objects, or signaling dangers.

In conjunction with the visual elements, audio elements bring the game world to life and deepen the player's immersion. Sound effects play a vital role in providing auditory feedback and enhancing the player's engagement with the game. Footstep sounds, combat noises, environmental audio, and interactive cues provide important information about the player's actions, surroundings, and the consequences of their choices. The use of spatial audio techniques, such as stereo sound, surround sound, or even 3D audio, can further enhance the sense of immersion and realism.

Music is another essential component of the audio design in a game. A well-composed soundtrack complements the gameplay, evokes emotions, and enhances the overall experience. Music can set the mood for different scenes, build tension during intense moments, create a sense of wonder during exploration, or provide a triumphant score during important milestones. The melodies, harmonies, and rhythms of the music can leave a lasting impression on players, becoming deeply associated with the game and evoking nostalgia long after they've played it.

The combination of art and audio elements in a game serves multiple purposes. They contribute to the storytelling and narrative by visually depicting characters, events, and settings, as well as providing voice acting, dialogues, and sound effects that bring the story to life. These elements work together to create memorable and impactful moments that resonate with players emotionally. Furthermore, the art and audio design provide important gameplay feedback, offering visual and auditory cues that guide players, inform them about their progress, and alert them to important events or changes in the game world.

Ultimately, the art and audio in a game serve as powerful tools to engage players, draw them into the game world, and heighten their overall experience. By carefully designing and integrating these elements, game designers can create a seamless and immersive player journey that leaves a lasting impression.

Chapter 7 - Quality Assurance and Testing

Quality Assurance and Testing play a crucial role in the development of video games, ensuring that the final product meets high standards of quality, functionality, and player satisfaction. As games designers strive to bring their creative vision to life, it is essential to have a robust testing process in place to identify and address any issues or bugs that may affect the gameplay experience.

In the world of game development, quality assurance refers to the systematic process of checking and evaluating various aspects of a game, including its functionality, performance, stability, and overall user experience. Game designers work closely with quality assurance teams to define and establish testing methodologies, strategies, and standards that align with the project's objectives. They collaborate to create test plans and scenarios that thoroughly examine different aspects of the game, such as gameplay mechanics, level design, controls, audiovisual elements, and user interface.

Testing is a vital component of quality assurance, involving the actual execution of test cases and the identification of any defects or issues within the game. Games designers actively participate in this process, collaborating with testers to understand and address reported problems. They provide valuable insights into the design intent, gameplay mechanics, and overall player experience, assisting in the effective resolution of identified issues. This collaborative effort ensures that the game is thoroughly evaluated from a design perspective, allowing for necessary adjustments to be made to enhance the overall quality and polish.

Furthermore, quality assurance and testing also help games designers in identifying potential gameplay imbalances, glitches, or other issues that may arise during the player's journey. By thoroughly testing the game, designers gain valuable feedback that allows them to fine-tune and refine the gameplay mechanics, pacing, and difficulty levels. This iterative process helps in delivering a more enjoyable and engaging experience for players.

Overall, quality assurance and testing are essential components of the game development process, enabling games designers to identify and address issues that may impact the player experience. By actively participating in the testing phase, designers can ensure that their creative vision aligns with the expectations of players, resulting in a polished and high-quality game that captivates and entertains its audience.

The importance of quality assurance (QA) in game development

Quality assurance is absolutely vital in games design for a multitude of reasons. It serves as a critical process to ensure that a game meets the highest standards of quality, functionality, and player satisfaction. By conducting comprehensive testing and evaluation, game designers can identify and address potential issues and defects before the game is unleashed upon eager players.

When quality assurance falls short, it can have significant repercussions. Perhaps the most noticeable consequence is a negative player experience. Gamers expect games to be seamless, immersive, and enjoyable. If a game is released without proper testing, it can be plagued by frustrating glitches, game-breaking bugs, or imbalanced gameplay. These issues can seriously diminish the player's enjoyment and satisfaction, resulting in unfavourable reviews, disgruntled players, and a tarnished reputation for the game and the development studio.

Furthermore, inadequate quality assurance can have financial implications. Releasing a game riddled with critical issues may lead to a surge of customer complaints, refund requests, and even legal consequences. Poor quality can damage the studio's reputation, making it difficult to attract players and secure future projects. It may also require costly post-release updates and patches to rectify the identified issues, necessitating additional resources and expenses that could have been avoided through proper testing.

In addition to these practical consequences, quality assurance plays a pivotal role in maintaining the credibility and professionalism of the game development industry. Players have high expectations for the games they invest their time and money in, and consistent lack of quality can undermine their trust in the industry as a whole. This can have far-reaching implications, affecting the success and sustainability of individual studios and the broader gaming community.

In a nutshell, ensuring high-quality assurance is a fundamental aspect of games design. By devoting time and resources to rigorous testing and quality control, game designers can deliver exceptional gaming experiences that meet player expectations, mitigate potential issues, and establish a strong reputation for excellence in the industry. Ultimately, the pursuit of quality assurance is not just about meeting industry standards, but about delivering joy, satisfaction, and unforgettable experiences to gamers around the world.

Developing a robust testing process and bug tracking system

Developing a robust testing process and bug tracking system is crucial for games designers to ensure the quality and stability of their games. It involves creating a structured and comprehensive approach to identify, track, and resolve bugs and issues throughout the development cycle.

Firstly, games designers establish a testing plan that outlines the scope, objectives, and methodologies for testing. This includes defining the target platforms, test cases, and the team responsible for executing the tests. They identify key areas of the game that require thorough testing, such as gameplay mechanics, user interface, performance, and compatibility.

Next, a bug tracking system is implemented to efficiently track and manage identified issues. This system typically consists of a database or software that allows the team to log, prioritize, and assign bugs to the relevant team members. It helps ensure that bugs are properly documented, tracked, and resolved in a timely manner.

For example, let's consider a scenario where a game designer is working on a role-playing game (RPG). They would create a testing process that includes rigorous playtesting to ensure the game mechanics, combat system, quests, and character progression are functioning as intended. They might also conduct compatibility testing on different platforms and devices to ensure a smooth gaming experience for players.

To develop a bug tracking system, the game designer might use dedicated bug tracking software or project management tools with built-in bug tracking capabilities. They would set up categories and priorities for bugs, assign them to appropriate team members (e.g., programmers, artists), and track the progress of bug fixes. The system would also include features for attaching relevant files, adding comments, and generating reports for efficient communication and documentation.

Throughout the testing process, games designers collaborate closely with the development team, providing clear and detailed bug reports with reproducible steps and accompanying assets when necessary. They regularly communicate with programmers, artists, and other stakeholders to ensure bugs are addressed promptly and effectively. This iterative feedback loop between the games designer and the development team is essential for refining and improving the game's quality.

By implementing a robust testing process and bug tracking system, games designers can effectively identify, track, and resolve issues, ensuring a higher level of quality and polish in the final game. It allows for efficient collaboration, enhances communication, and enables the team to deliver a more stable and enjoyable gaming experience for players.

Example of bug tracking software games designers may use to track bugs

When it comes to tracking bugs during game creation, one popular software that games designers might use is "Jira." It's like a superhero sidekick that helps them stay organized and on top of all the pesky bugs that may creep into their game.

With Jira, games designers can easily log bug reports by providing detailed descriptions, steps to reproduce the issue, and even attaching helpful screenshots or videos. They can assign bugs to the right team members, set priorities and due dates, and keep track of the progress. It's like having a trusty assistant who knows exactly who's responsible for squashing those bugs.

Jira is also great at fostering collaboration and communication. Games designers can leave comments, tag team members, and receive notifications on updates and changes. It's like a virtual team hangout where everyone can work together to tackle those bugs head-on.

One of the coolest things about Jira is its customizable workflows. Games designers can create their own bug resolution stages, like "open," "in progress," "resolved," and "closed." They can even set up automatic transitions between these stages, making it a breeze to manage the bug fixing process.

But it doesn't stop there! Jira also offers handy reporting and analytics features. Games designers can generate reports and metrics to gain insights into bug trends, spot recurring issues, and keep a close eye on the overall progress of bug fixing. It's like having a superpower that helps them make informed decisions and ensure their game is top-notch.

Of course, Jira is just one of the bug tracking software options out there. There are other friendly helpers like Bugzilla, Trello, Asana, or Hansoft that games designers can choose from. It all depends on their team's preferences and the unique needs of their game development studio. So, they can find their perfect bug-tracking sidekick and create the best game possible!

Playtesting and gathering user feedback

Games designers playtest and gather user feedback during the game design process to ensure the game meets players' expectations and provides an enjoyable experience. They employ various techniques and use tools/software to facilitate this important step.

One common technique is conducting playtesting sessions with real players. Games designers organize playtesting sessions where individuals or groups are invited to play the game and provide feedback. This can be done in-person or remotely, depending on the circumstances. During playtesting, designers observe players' interactions, note their reactions, and collect feedback through surveys, interviews, or focus group discussions.

To facilitate the playtesting process, games designers often use specialized playtesting software and tools. These tools allow them to capture gameplay footage, record player actions, and collect data on player behaviour. Examples of popular playtesting tools include PlaytestCloud, UserTesting, and Lookback. These tools provide valuable insights into how players engage with the game, identify pain points, and highlight areas for improvement.

In addition to dedicated playtesting tools, games designers may also use general-purpose software for data collection and analysis. Spreadsheets, survey tools like Google Forms or SurveyMonkey, and collaboration platforms such as Trello or Slack can be employed to gather and organize user feedback. These tools help designers track and categorize feedback, identify patterns, and prioritize areas of improvement.

Moreover, some game developers leverage analytics software or services to gather quantitative data about player behaviour. These tools provide detailed metrics on gameplay patterns, session length, player progression, and more. Examples of popular analytics tools for games include Unity Analytics,

Google Analytics for Games, or GameAnalytics. By analyzing these metrics, designers gain insights into how players engage with the game, identify bottlenecks, and make informed decisions for enhancing the gameplay experience.

Ultimately, the goal of playtesting and gathering user feedback is to iterate and improve the game based on player insights. It allows games designers to address issues, refine mechanics, adjust difficulty levels, and ensure the game resonates with the intended audience. By actively involving players in the development process, games designers can create a game that captures the interest and enjoyment of the players, resulting in a more successful and satisfying gaming experience.

Iterating based on QA findings and refining the game's performance

When a games designer receives feedback and findings from quality assurance (QA) testing, they use this information to iterate and refine the game's performance. This iterative process is crucial for identifying and resolving issues, improving gameplay mechanics, and enhancing overall performance. Let's explore how games designers approach iteration based on QA findings and some techniques and software they utilize.

One common practice is to analyze QA reports and bug tracking systems. Games designers carefully review the reported bugs, issues, and performance bottlenecks to identify patterns and prioritize areas for improvement. They categorize the issues based on severity and impact on gameplay, allowing them to focus on critical aspects first.

To address these findings, games designers collaborate closely with programmers and developers. They provide detailed feedback, suggestions, and documentation to guide the necessary changes. For instance, if QA identifies a bug related to character movement, the games designer would communicate the specific issue, propose potential solutions, and work with the programming team to implement the necessary adjustments.

Prototyping and rapid iteration are essential techniques in refining the game's performance. Games designers often create small-scale prototypes or mock-ups to test and fine-tune specific gameplay mechanics, controls, or performance-related aspects. These prototypes help identify potential issues early on and allow for rapid experimentation and adjustment. Games designers may use prototyping software such as Unity, Unreal Engine, or GameMaker Studio, which provide tools and frameworks for creating and testing prototypes efficiently.

In terms of performance optimization, games designers collaborate closely with the programming and technical teams. They analyze performance metrics, such as frame rate, loading times, and memory usage, to identify areas where optimizations are needed. For example, if QA reports performance issues during intense combat scenes, the games designer would work with programmers to optimize the rendering, physics, or AI systems to ensure smoother gameplay.

Furthermore, games designers may leverage performance profiling tools and software to identify specific performance bottlenecks. These tools, such as Intel GPA, NVIDIA Nsight, or Unity Profiler, provide detailed insights into resource usage, CPU/GPU performance, and memory allocation. By analyzing this data, games designers can pinpoint areas that require optimization and work closely with the programming team to implement necessary changes.

Throughout the iterative process, games designers constantly playtest and gather feedback to validate the effectiveness of their refinements. They organize internal playtesting sessions or involve external testers to evaluate the game's performance improvements and address any remaining issues. This continuous feedback loop helps ensure that the game's performance and overall experience meet the desired standards.

In summary, games designers iterate based on QA findings by analyzing reports, collaborating with programmers, and utilizing prototyping techniques. They employ performance profiling tools and software to optimize the game's performance and collaborate closely with the development team. By combining these approaches, games designers refine gameplay mechanics, resolve issues, and enhance the overall performance and quality of the game.

Chapter 8 - Launch and Post-Production

"Launch and Post-Production" is a phase in game development that occurs after the game has been completed and is ready for release. For games designers, this phase involves activities and responsibilities related to the successful launch of the game and its continued support and improvement in the post-release period.

Let's explore what it means to a games designer in more detail.

Launch Preparation: Games designers play a vital role in preparing the game for launch. They work closely with the development team to ensure that all aspects of the game, including gameplay mechanics, levels, audiovisual elements, and performance, are polished and ready for the intended audience. They collaborate with marketing and PR teams to create promotional materials, trailers, and press releases that effectively communicate the game's features and appeal to the target market.

Release Management: Games designers contribute to the overall release management process. They coordinate with producers, project managers, and other team members to plan and execute the launch strategy, including setting release dates, coordinating distribution on different platforms, and ensuring compatibility with various hardware configurations. They may also work on post-release updates and patches to address any immediate issues or add new features based on player feedback.

Player Feedback and Support: After the game's launch, games designers actively engage with the player community to gather feedback, address concerns, and provide support. They monitor player forums, social media channels, and review platforms to understand player sentiments, identify recurring issues, and collect suggestions for future updates or improvements. They collaborate with the development team to prioritize and implement necessary changes or bug fixes based on this feedback.

Post-Release Content and Updates: Games designers are involved in the creation and release of post-launch content, such as downloadable content (DLC), expansions, or updates. They contribute to the design and implementation of new levels, characters, gameplay features, or storylines that enhance the game's longevity and offer additional value to players. They work with artists, programmers, and other team members to ensure seamless integration of new content into the existing game world.

Data Analysis and Iteration: Games designers utilize player data and analytics to gain insights into player behaviour, engagement, and preferences. They analyze gameplay metrics, such as playtime, completion rates, or in-game purchases, to understand how players interact with the game and identify areas for improvement. This data-driven approach helps games designers refine existing mechanics, introduce balancing adjustments, or develop new content that aligns with player interests.

Community Engagement: Games designers actively engage with the game's community, fostering a positive and interactive relationship with players. They participate in forums, social media discussions, and live events to gather feedback, answer questions, and provide insights into game design decisions. By maintaining a strong connection with the player community, games designers can better understand their needs, build brand loyalty, and drive ongoing interest in the game.

"Launch and Post-Production" is the phase in game development where games designers focus on the successful release of the game, gathering player feedback, providing support, and driving ongoing improvements and content updates. Their responsibilities include launch preparation, release management, player feedback analysis, post-release content creation, data-driven iteration, and community engagement. By effectively managing this phase, games designers contribute to the long-term success and enjoyment of the game.

Preparing the game for launch: marketing and distribution

When it comes to preparing a game for launch, games designers play a crucial role in the marketing and distribution process. It's all about getting the game out there and getting players excited to play it. Here's how they do it:

First, games designers team up with the marketing folks to figure out who the game is for. They dive into the game's genre, mechanics, and style to determine the ideal audience. This helps them create marketing strategies that will resonate with the right people.

Next, they work with artists and designers to create stunning visuals that showcase the game's awesomeness. Think logos, screenshots, trailers, and more. These assets make people go, "Wow, I want to play that game!"

Then, they join forces with the marketing team to come up with a solid plan. This involves deciding where and how to promote the game, whether it's through social media, gaming websites, conventions, or partnering with influencers. They want to make sure they reach as many interested players as possible.

Timing is important too. Games designers coordinate with producers, project managers, and publishers to pick the perfect release date and the platforms the game will be available on. They consider factors like market trends and competition to maximize the game's impact.

As the big day approaches, games designers get the game ready for distribution. They work closely with the development team to package the game and ensure it meets all the platform requirements. They want to make sure players can easily access and enjoy the game on their chosen platforms.

But it doesn't stop there. Games designers also engage with the gaming community. They participate in forums, social media chats, and events, sharing updates and listening to feedback. They want players to feel involved and excited about the game's release.

They also work closely with the marketing team to coordinate press and review campaigns. They provide information, early access, and interviews to journalists, influencers, and content creators. The goal is to generate positive buzz and build anticipation.

Before the official launch, games designers gather feedback from playtesting and community interactions. They listen to what players have to say, identify areas for improvement, and make necessary tweaks to enhance the game. They want to ensure the game meets players' expectations and delivers an amazing experience.

By working their magic in the marketing and distribution process, games designers help build excitement, connect with players, and set the stage for a successful launch. It's all about sharing the joy of gaming with as many people as possible!

Creating promotional materials and trailers

Games designers play a super important role in creating awesome promotional materials and trailers for the games they've created. These materials are like the game's shining armour, designed to catch everyone's attention and make them go, "Wow, I need to play this game!" Here's how games designers bring the magic to this process:

Game Love: Games designers have a deep love for the game they've created. They know every nook and cranny, from the quirky characters to the mind-blowing mechanics. With their passion and knowledge, they pick out the coolest features to show off in the promotional materials.

Artistic Avengers: Games designers team up with talented artists and graphic designers, like a superhero squad, to create visuals that will knock your socks off. They work together to make sure the graphics perfectly capture the game's unique style and make your eyes sparkle with excitement.

Storytelling Sorcery: Games designers are masters of storytelling. They cook up a captivating narrative for the promotional materials, weaving a tale that will leave you hungry for more. It's like they cast a spell that hooks you in and makes you crave the game's thrilling adventure.

Gameplay Galore: Games designers carefully choose the most thrilling gameplay moments to showcase in the materials. They work their magic to capture the most epic battles, mind-bending puzzles, and heart-pounding action, all in a way that makes you scream, "I must play this game NOW!"

Editing Extravaganza: Games designers collaborate with video editors and sound designers to make the promotional materials shine like a shooting star. They add special effects, snappy transitions, and music that gives you goosebumps. It's like they sprinkle stardust on the footage to make it even more captivating.

Marketing Marvels: Games designers team up with the marketing folks to make sure the materials align with the overall marketing strategy. They want to make sure the materials hit the right target and speak directly to the hearts of potential players. It's all about creating that buzz and getting people excited!

Never-ending Improvements: Games designers love feedback! They gather input from the development team, playtesters, and marketing geniuses to make the materials even better. They're like master chefs, adjusting the recipe until it's just right, ensuring that the materials do justice to the game.

With their passion, artistic collaborations, storytelling skills, and a pinch of marketing magic, games designers create promotional materials and trailers that leave everyone in awe. They're the superheroes who make you go, "I can't wait to dive into this incredible game adventure!"

Dealing with the launch day and managing player

feedback

Games designers play a crucial role in managing the launch day of a new game they have designed, as well as handling player feedback that comes pouring in.

Here's how they tackle these challenges with finesse:

Launch Preparation: Games designers work closely with the development team to ensure that the game is polished, bug-free, and ready for launch. They perform thorough testing and quality assurance to catch any last-minute issues and make necessary adjustments. They also coordinate with marketing and PR teams to create a buzz around the game, generating excitement and anticipation among players.

Launch Day Monitoring: On the big day, games designers keep a close eye on the game's release, monitoring player feedback, and ensuring a smooth launch. They may work closely with programmers and support teams to address any technical issues that players may encounter. Their goal is to provide a positive and seamless experience for players as they embark on their gaming journey.

Community Engagement: Games designers actively engage with the player community, whether it's through forums, social media platforms, or dedicated game websites. They listen to player feedback, answer questions, and address concerns. By maintaining an open and transparent line of communication, they build trust and foster a sense of community around the game.

Feedback Analysis: Games designers carefully analyze player feedback, paying attention to both positive and negative comments. They identify common issues, gather valuable insights, and use this feedback to improve the game. They may collaborate with the development team to prioritize and implement necessary changes through patches or updates.

Player Support: Games designers work hand in hand with customer support teams to assist players with any issues or inquiries they may have. They ensure that players receive timely and helpful responses, resolving technical problems or addressing gameplay concerns. Their goal is to provide exceptional support and ensure that players have a positive experience with the game.

Continuous Updates and Improvements: Games designers remain dedicated to enhancing the game post-launch. They gather data on player behavior, engagement metrics, and feedback to inform future updates and content expansions. They strive to create a dynamic and evolving experience that keeps players engaged and excited for what's to come.

Throughout the launch period and beyond, games designers are at the forefront of managing player feedback, ensuring a smooth launch, and continuously improving the game. Their dedication to delivering a high-quality experience and their responsiveness to player input contribute to the long-term success of the game and the satisfaction of its players.

Post-launch support, updates, and expansion plans

After a game has been released, games designers play a crucial role in providing post-launch support, implementing updates, and planning expansions to keep the game fresh and engaging. Here's how they handle these aspects:

Player Feedback Analysis: Games designers actively monitor player feedback, reviews, and community discussions to understand player experiences and identify areas for improvement. They analyze the feedback to prioritize and address issues, bug fixes, and gameplay enhancements in future updates.

Patch and Update Releases: Games designers collaborate with the development team to plan and release patches and updates. They work on fixing reported bugs, addressing balance issues, and introducing new features or content. These updates help maintain player interest, improve the overall game experience, and demonstrate the team's commitment to ongoing support.

Expansion Planning: Games designers play a key role in expanding the game's content and features through expansions or DLC (downloadable content). They brainstorm and develop new ideas for additional levels, characters, quests, or game modes, keeping in mind the game's theme and player preferences. They work closely with artists, level designers, and programmers to bring these expansion plans to life.

Balancing and Fine-tuning: Games designers continuously assess and fine-tune gameplay mechanics, difficulty levels, and balance to ensure an enjoyable experience for both new and existing players. They analyze player data, engagement metrics, and feedback to make informed decisions about adjusting game elements and enhancing the overall game experience.

Community Engagement: Games designers actively engage with the player community through social media, forums, and other platforms. They provide updates, communicate upcoming features or expansions, and respond to player inquiries. By fostering a strong relationship with the community, they build player loyalty and create a sense of shared ownership in the game's development.

Long-term Roadmap: Games designers work with the development team and stakeholders to create a long-term roadmap for the game. They plan major updates, expansions, or sequels to extend the game's lifespan and maintain player interest. They consider market trends, player feedback, and business goals to make informed decisions about the game's future direction.

By providing post-launch support, regular updates, and well-planned expansions, games designers ensure that the game continues to evolve and meet player expectations even after its initial release. Their ongoing dedication to improving the game's quality and engaging with the player community contributes to its long-term success and player satisfaction.

Chapter 9 - The Business of Game Design

When it comes to game design, it's not all just fun and games - there's a business side to it too! The business of game design involves understanding the market, making smart decisions, and ensuring the game's commercial success. As a games designer, you need to balance your creative ideas with a keen sense of the market to turn your passion into a sustainable career.

In the exciting world of game design, it's essential to keep your finger on the pulse of the industry. That means researching the target audience, staying up-to-date with the latest trends, and finding unique ways to captivate players. By understanding what players want and what makes a game stand out, you can create experiences that gamers will love.

Working closely with producers, publishers, and stakeholders is also part of the game designer's business toolkit. Together, you'll align your creative vision with the project's budget, scope, and timelines. By collaborating effectively, you can ensure that your artistic vision comes to life while meeting the practical needs of the project.

Financial savvy is another important skill for game designers. Budgeting, resource management, and cost control are all essential to keep your project on track. By tracking expenses, managing contracts, and exploring different revenue streams, like in-game purchases or expansions, you can make sure your game not only shines creatively but also makes financial sense.

Knowing the legal and intellectual property aspects of the industry is also vital. Copyright, licensing, and publishing agreements protect your hard work and ensure that you're playing by the rules.

By balancing your creative genius with a business mindset,

you'll be able to navigate the industry successfully. So, get ready to create amazing games that capture players' hearts while also ensuring your career as a game designer is a prosperous one!

Overview of the game industry's landscape

The game industry's landscape is a dynamic and thriving ecosystem that encompasses a wide range of sectors, platforms, and players.

Here's a detailed overview of its key components:

Platforms: Games are available on various platforms, including consoles (such as PlayStation, Xbox, and Nintendo), PC, mobile devices, and virtual reality (VR) platforms. Each platform offers unique opportunities and challenges for game developers.

Genres: Games span a wide range of genres, catering to diverse player preferences. Popular genres include action, adventure, role-playing, strategy, sports, puzzle, and simulation. Each genre offers distinct gameplay mechanics and experiences.

Market Size: The game industry is a multibillion-dollar market, with a growing global audience. The market size is influenced by factors such as technological advancements, accessibility, and the popularity of gaming as a form of entertainment.

Players: Gamers come from various demographics and include both casual and hardcore players. The player base is expanding, encompassing people of all ages and backgrounds. The rise of mobile gaming has contributed to a more diverse player profile.

Development Studios: Game development studios range from small indie teams to large multinational companies. They are responsible for creating games, employing a diverse range of talent, including game designers, artists, programmers, sound designers, and producers.

Distribution Channels: Games can be distributed through various channels, including digital marketplaces (such as Steam, PlayStation Store, App Store, and Google Play), physical copies (discs/cartridges), and subscription-based services (like Xbox Game Pass or PlayStation Plus).

Monetization Models: Game monetization has evolved beyond the traditional one-time purchase model. Developers now employ various models, including free-to-play with in-app purchases, subscription-based models, downloadable content (DLC), and micro-transactions. These models generate revenue while offering different player experiences.

Esports and Competitive Gaming: Esports has emerged as a significant sector within the game industry. Professional players compete in organized tournaments, attracting large audiences and sponsorships. Esports titles and related content have become a significant revenue driver.

Indie Games: The rise of indie games has brought fresh perspectives, innovative gameplay mechanics, and unique art styles to the industry. Independent developers often have more creative freedom and can cater to niche audiences.

Technology and Innovation: The game industry is heavily influenced by technological advancements. Cutting-edge technologies like virtual reality, augmented reality, cloud gaming, and artificial intelligence are shaping the future of game design and player experiences.

Global Market: The game industry has a global reach, with games being developed and enjoyed by people around the world. Cultural diversity, localization efforts, and international markets play a significant role in game development and distribution.

Industry Events and Communities: Various industry events, such as game expos, conferences, and awards shows, bring together professionals, enthusiasts, and players to showcase upcoming games, share knowledge, and celebrate the industry's achievements.

The game industry's landscape is constantly evolving, driven by technological advancements, changing player preferences, and market dynamics. It offers a vibrant and exciting environment for game designers to unleash their creativity and contribute to the ever-growing world of interactive entertainment.

Monetization models and revenue streams

Monetization models and revenue streams in game design refer to the different ways in which game developers generate income from their games. Here are some common monetization models and revenue streams:

One-Time Purchase: This traditional model involves selling the game to players for a fixed price. Once players purchase the game, they have full access to its content without any additional charges.

Free-to-Play (F2P): In the free-to-play model, the game is available to download and play for free. However, developers generate revenue through in-app purchases (IAPs) or micro-transactions, where players can buy virtual goods, cosmetic items, additional levels, or other premium features within the game.

Subscription Model: Some games offer a subscription-based model, where players pay a recurring fee (monthly or annually) to access the game and its content. This model often provides additional benefits, such as exclusive in-game items, early access to new content, or premium features.

Advertising: Advertising is a revenue stream commonly used in mobile games and free-to-play titles. Developers integrate advertisements within the game, such as banner ads, interstitial ads, or rewarded video ads. Ad revenue is generated based on impressions, clicks, or completed views.

In-Game Purchases: This revenue stream involves offering players the option to purchase virtual goods, currency, or items directly within the game. These purchases enhance the gameplay experience, provide convenience, or offer cosmetic enhancements.

Downloadable Content (DLC): DLC refers to additional content released after the game's initial launch, which players can purchase to expand or enhance their gameplay experience. DLC may include new levels, characters, storylines, or features.

Season Passes: Season passes allow players to pre-purchase a bundle of upcoming DLC or expansions at a discounted price. Players gain access to future content as it becomes available without additional charges.

Sponsorships and Partnerships: Developers may enter into sponsorship or partnership agreements with brands or advertisers. This can involve featuring branded content, product placements, or cross-promotions within the game, generating revenue through these collaborations.

Crowdfunding: Crowdfunding platforms like Kickstarter or Indiegogo enable developers to raise funds from the community to develop their games. Backers contribute money in exchange for rewards, early access, or exclusive content.

Esports and Competitive Gaming: Revenue can be generated through organized esports tournaments, where players compete for prizes and sponsorships. Esports events attract audiences, advertising, and partnerships, contributing to revenue streams.

Licensing and Merchandising: Successful games often expand their revenue streams by licensing intellectual property rights for merchandise, such as toys, apparel, collectibles, or even adaptations into other media formats like movies or TV shows.

It's important for game designers to carefully consider the monetization models and revenue streams that align with their game's target audience, genre, and gameplay experience. Balancing the need for revenue generation with player satisfaction and fairness is crucial for maintaining a positive relationship with the player base.

Navigating intellectual property and copyright issues

Games designers navigate intellectual property (IP) and copyright issues by embracing the importance of originality and respecting the creative rights of others.

Here's a friendly overview of how they tackle these matters:

Embracing Creativity: Games designers thrive on creating unique and imaginative game concepts, characters, and worlds. They pour their creativity into crafting original experiences that captivate players and stand out from the crowd.

Respecting IP Rights: Games designers understand the significance of intellectual property rights and make a conscious effort to avoid infringing upon the copyrighted works of others. They value the contributions of fellow creators and strive to build upon their own original ideas.

Licensing Collaboration: Games designers may collaborate with artists, musicians, and other creatives to bring their game to life. They establish clear agreements and obtain necessary licenses to use copyrighted materials, ensuring that everyone's rights and contributions are protected.

Copyright Clearance: Games designers undertake a diligent clearance process to identify any potential infringements within their game's content. They review artwork, music, text, and other elements to ensure they have the proper permissions or have created their own original material.

Fair Use Considerations: Games designers are aware of fair use guidelines, which allow limited use of copyrighted material for purposes such as commentary, criticism, or parody. They exercise caution and seek legal advice when determining if their use falls within the realm of fair use.

Trademark Protection: Games designers may seek trademark protection for their game titles, logos, or distinctive brand identities. This safeguards their unique branding elements and prevents confusion in the market, ensuring players can easily identify their games.

Compliance with DMCA: Games designers comply with the Digital Millennium Copyright Act (DMCA) regulations, which outline procedures for addressing copyright infringement claims. They respect the rights of content creators and promptly respond to legitimate claims while following the proper procedures.

Legal Guidance: To navigate the intricate world of intellectual property and copyright, games designers consult with legal professionals who specialize in this area. They seek expert advice to ensure their games adhere to relevant laws, protecting their own intellectual property and respecting the rights of others.

By embracing originality, respecting intellectual property rights, obtaining necessary licenses, and seeking legal guidance when needed, games designers maintain a creative and lawful approach to game development. They contribute to a vibrant and ethical gaming industry where innovation thrives, and everyone's creative rights are upheld.

Building a sustainable career as a game designer

Building a sustainable career as a game designer requires a combination of passion, skill development, adaptability, and a deep understanding of the industry.

Here are some points on how to achieve this goal:

Continuous Skill Development: Game designers should always strive to enhance their skills and stay updated with the latest trends and technologies in the industry. They can pursue formal education in game design, participate in workshops, attend conferences, and engage in self-directed learning to expand their knowledge and expertise.

Building a Portfolio: A strong portfolio is essential for showcasing one's talent and creativity to potential employers or clients. Game designers should create a diverse range of projects, including personal game prototypes, level designs, or concept art, and ensure their portfolio reflects their abilities and unique style.

Networking and Collaboration: Building a network of professional contacts in the game industry is crucial for career growth. Game designers can attend industry events, join online forums and communities, and actively engage with fellow designers, artists, programmers, and industry experts. Collaborating on projects and exchanging ideas can open doors to new opportunities and foster professional growth.

Gaining Practical Experience: Practical experience is invaluable in the game design field. Game designers can seek internships, participate in game jams, or contribute to indie game projects to gain hands-on experience and expand their understanding of the development process. Practical experience not only helps build skills but also demonstrates a commitment to the industry.

Adaptability and Versatility: The game industry is dynamic, and game designers need to be adaptable to changing trends and technologies. They should be open to learning new tools, techniques, and design philosophies. Additionally, possessing a versatile skill set, such as proficiency in multiple game engines, programming languages, or art styles, can make game designers more marketable and adaptable to various project requirements.

Seeking Mentorship: Finding a mentor who has experience in the game industry can provide invaluable guidance and insights. Mentors can offer advice, critique work, and provide career guidance to help game designers navigate challenges and make informed decisions throughout their career.

Entrepreneurial Mindset: Game designers can also explore entrepreneurship by developing their own games or establishing independent studios. This requires a combination of creative vision, business acumen, and the ability to manage resources effectively. Entrepreneurship allows game designers to have more control over their creative work and opens up opportunities for self-publishing and revenue generation.

Professionalism and Work Ethic: Building a sustainable career as a game designer requires professionalism, reliability, and a strong work ethic. Meeting deadlines, communicating effectively, collaborating with team members, and delivering high-quality work consistently are all essential aspects of establishing a positive reputation in the industry.

By continuously developing skills, building a strong portfolio, networking, gaining practical experience, being adaptable, seeking mentorship, embracing entrepreneurship, and demonstrating professionalism, game designers can build a sustainable and fulfilling career in the exciting and ever-evolving field of game design.

Chapter 10 - Challenges and Future Trends

Challenges and future trends in game design present exciting opportunities and complexities for game designers to navigate. As the gaming industry continues to evolve, new challenges emerge, pushing designers to explore innovative solutions and push boundaries.

Here are some points highlighting the challenges and future trends in game design:

Evolving Player Expectations: One of the significant challenges in game design is meeting the ever-evolving expectations of players. As technology advances and players become more discerning, they crave immersive experiences, captivating narratives, and engaging gameplay mechanics. Game designers must constantly strive to create unique and innovative experiences that captivate and satisfy players, pushing the boundaries of what is possible in game design.

Emerging Technologies: The rapid advancement of technologies such as virtual reality (VR), augmented reality (AR), and cloud gaming presents both opportunities and challenges for game designers. Embracing these technologies requires designers to understand their potential and limitations, adapt their design approach, and explore new ways of crafting immersive and interactive experiences. Designers must also consider the impact of emerging technologies on gameplay mechanics, user interfaces, and player interactions.

Inclusivity and Diversity: The game industry is increasingly recognizing the importance of inclusivity and diversity in game design. Game designers are challenged to create experiences that cater to a broader audience, representing diverse cultures, genders, abilities, and backgrounds. This involves not only diverse character representation but also designing gameplay mechanics and narratives that resonate with a wide range of players. Game designers play a crucial role in fostering inclusivity and promoting positive representation within the gaming community.

Ethical Considerations: As games become more immersive and realistic, game designers must address ethical considerations in their design choices. This includes topics such as player well-being, responsible monetization practices, avoiding harmful stereotypes, and promoting positive social impact. Designers must balance the desire for engaging gameplay with ensuring player safety, mental health, and overall positive experiences.

Data-driven Design: With the growth of online and multiplayer games, data-driven design is becoming increasingly important. Game designers are using player data and analytics to inform their design decisions, optimize gameplay mechanics, and personalize experiences. However, this also raises concerns about player privacy, data ethics, and the balance between data-driven design and maintaining creative freedom.

Sustainability and Social Responsibility: The gaming industry is also embracing sustainability and social responsibility as important considerations in game design. This involves minimizing the environmental impact of game development, promoting diversity and inclusion, and addressing social issues through meaningful narratives and gameplay mechanics. Game designers have the power to create games that not only entertain but also educate, inspire, and drive positive change.

Navigating these challenges and embracing future trends requires game designers to be adaptable, innovative, and empathetic to the needs and desires of players. By staying informed about industry trends, engaging in ongoing learning, collaborating with diverse teams, and thinking critically about the impact of their designs, game designers can shape the future of gaming and create experiences that resonate with players around the world.

Embracing emerging technologies (VR, AR, AI)

Game designers have embraced emerging technologies like Virtual Reality (VR), Augmented Reality (AR), and Artificial Intelligence (AI) to revolutionize the gaming industry and enhance player experiences. Here are some ways game designers have leveraged these technologies:

Virtual Reality (VR): VR technology immerses players in a virtual environment, providing a highly interactive and immersive experience. Game designers have created VR games that allow players to explore virtual worlds, interact with objects and characters, and experience a heightened sense of presence. They design gameplay mechanics and user interfaces specifically tailored for VR, leveraging the technology to create innovative and captivating experiences.

Augmented Reality (AR): AR overlays digital elements onto the real world, blending virtual and real-life experiences. Game designers have utilized AR to create mobile games that merge digital content with the player's environment. These games often encourage physical movement, exploration, and real-time interaction with virtual objects. AR games have transformed the way players engage with their surroundings, turning everyday spaces into magical gaming environments.

Artificial Intelligence (AI): AI technology has enabled game designers to create more immersive and intelligent game experiences. AI-driven characters and enemies can exhibit realistic behaviours, adapt to player actions, and provide dynamic challenges. Game designers use AI algorithms to enhance non-player characters (NPCs), optimize enemy behaviours, and create more engaging and realistic gameplay scenarios. AI can also be utilized for procedural content generation, generating dynamic levels, quests, or game elements to provide endless replayability.

Enhanced Gameplay Mechanics: Emerging technologies have expanded the possibilities for gameplay mechanics. For example, game designers have used VR to introduce innovative locomotion systems, intuitive hand tracking, and immersive gesture-based interactions. AR has allowed for location-based gameplay and real-world object recognition. AI-driven algorithms have enabled dynamic decision-making by NPCs, realistic physics simulations, and adaptive difficulty scaling based on player performance.

New Design Paradigms: Emerging technologies have challenged traditional design paradigms, encouraging game designers to think outside the box. VR and AR have prompted the exploration of new narrative structures, spatial puzzles, and collaborative multiplayer experiences. AI-driven procedural generation has enabled the creation of vast and procedurally generated game worlds, offering unique experiences with each playthrough. These technologies have pushed the boundaries of game design, allowing for more innovative and immersive experiences.

Game designers continue to embrace emerging technologies to push the boundaries of interactive entertainment. They constantly explore ways to integrate VR, AR, and AI into their game designs, creating experiences that blur the line between reality and the virtual world. By harnessing these technologies, game designers aim to provide players with captivating, immersive, and transformative gaming experiences.

Exploring the future of game design and industry evolution

As game designers look toward the future, they are excited about the evolving landscape of game design and the industry as a whole.

Here are some key areas that game designers are exploring and trends that are shaping the future of game design:

Immersive Technologies: Game designers are embracing emerging technologies like Virtual Reality (VR), Augmented Reality (AR), and Mixed Reality (MR). These technologies offer unprecedented levels of immersion and interactivity, allowing players to become fully immersed in virtual worlds or overlay digital elements onto the real world. Game designers are constantly pushing the boundaries of these technologies to create more immersive and engaging experiences.

Cross-Platform and Cross-Play: With the increasing popularity of mobile gaming and the rise of cloud gaming, game designers are focusing on creating experiences that seamlessly span multiple platforms. Cross-platform games allow players to enjoy the same game on different devices, such as consoles, PCs, and mobile devices, ensuring a consistent experience regardless of the platform. Cross-play enables players on different platforms to play together, fostering a more inclusive and interconnected gaming community.

Player-Generated Content and Modding: Game designers are recognizing the value of player creativity and are incorporating systems that allow players to create and share their own content within games. This includes level editors, modding tools, and user-generated content platforms. By empowering players to be creators, game designers can extend the lifespan of games, promote community engagement, and foster a sense of ownership among players.

Procedural Generation and AI-Assisted Design: Procedural generation, combined with AI algorithms, offers game designers a powerful tool for creating vast and dynamic game worlds. By using algorithms to generate content such as levels, landscapes, quests, and narratives, game designers can provide players with unique and personalized experiences. AI-assisted design can also help with automating certain aspects of game development, such as generating animations or optimizing game mechanics.

Social and Community-driven Experiences: Game designers are focusing on creating games that foster social interactions and community engagement. This includes multiplayer experiences, shared world environments, and collaborative gameplay. With the rise of live service games, game designers are continually updating and expanding their games based on player feedback and community-driven initiatives.

Ethical and Inclusive Design: As the gaming industry becomes more diverse and inclusive, game designers are paying greater attention to ethical design practices and inclusivity. They are striving to create games that represent a wide range of cultures, perspectives, and identities. This includes addressing issues such as diversity, representation, accessibility, and responsible monetization practices.

Data-Driven Design and Personalization: Game designers are leveraging data analytics and player insights to inform their design decisions. By analyzing player behavior and preferences, game designers can create personalized experiences tailored to individual players. This includes adaptive difficulty systems, personalized content recommendations, and dynamic storytelling.

Sustainability and Environmental Consciousness: Game designers are increasingly incorporating sustainable practices into their designs, considering the environmental impact of game development and promoting eco-friendly initiatives. This includes optimizing resource usage, reducing carbon footprint, and exploring renewable energy sources for server infrastructure.

Indie and Alternative Game Development: The indie game scene continues to thrive, offering unique and innovative game experiences outside of mainstream productions. Game designers are embracing the freedom and creativity of indie development, exploring new genres, experimental mechanics, and unconventional storytelling approaches.

As the game industry evolves, game designers are at the forefront of shaping the future of interactive entertainment. They are pushing boundaries, embracing emerging technologies, fostering inclusivity, and designing experiences that resonate with players on a deep and personal level. The future of game design holds endless possibilities, and game designers are excited to explore and redefine the boundaries of interactive storytelling, immersion, and player engagement.

Reflecting on the journey of creating a game from

scratch

When a games designer looks back on a completed game and reflects on the journey of creating it from scratch, a wave of emotions and feelings washes over them. Firstly, there is a profound sense of accomplishment and pride. They are filled with awe at the realization that their initial ideas and concepts have transformed into a tangible, interactive experience that engages players.

There is also a mix of nostalgia and sentimentality as they revisit the various stages of development. They recall the exhilarating moments of inspiration, the long hours of hard work and dedication, and the challenges they faced along the way. The designer is reminded of the perseverance and resilience required to bring their vision to life.

Reflection often brings a deep appreciation for the collaborative efforts and teamwork that made the game possible. The designer recognizes and acknowledges the contributions of fellow artists, programmers, sound designers, and other members of the development team. They are grateful for the support, expertise, and creative synergy that elevated the game to its full potential.

Amidst the reflection, there may be a sense of growth and personal evolution. The designer recognizes how their skills, knowledge, and artistic sensibilities have evolved throughout the game's creation. They appreciate the valuable lessons learned, both from successes and from the inevitable setbacks and challenges faced. Reflecting on the journey allows them to celebrate their growth as a designer and gain insights that will shape future projects.

At the same time, there may be a touch of introspection and self-critique. The designer analyzes their work with a discerning eye, identifying areas for improvement or aspects they might approach differently in hindsight. However, this critical evaluation is balanced by a sense of satisfaction in knowing that they gave their all and created something meaningful.

In essence, reflecting on the journey of creating a game from scratch evokes a wide range of emotions for the games designer. It is a complex mix of pride, nostalgia, appreciation, growth, and self-evaluation. It is a moment to celebrate their achievements, learn from the process, and gather inspiration for future endeavours in the dynamic world of game design.

Encouraging aspiring game designers to pursue their passion

As a game designer, there are several ways to encourage and inspire other aspiring game designers to pursue their passion:

Share your story: Openly share your own journey as a game designer, including the challenges you faced, the lessons you learned, and the milestones you achieved. By sharing your personal experiences, you can provide valuable insights and inspiration to others who may be on a similar path.

Provide mentorship: Offer your guidance and support to aspiring game designers. Mentorship can take various forms, such as providing feedback on their work, sharing industry knowledge, or offering career advice. By serving as a mentor, you can help others navigate the complexities of game design and provide them with the confidence and encouragement they need to pursue their passion.

Showcase success stories: Highlight success stories of game designers who have achieved recognition or accomplished their goals. Whether it's through interviews, articles, or social media posts, sharing stories of other designers' accomplishments can serve as powerful motivation for aspiring game designers. It helps them see that their dreams are attainable and that hard work and dedication can lead to meaningful achievements.

Foster a supportive community: Create or contribute to a community where game designers can connect, collaborate, and share their experiences. This can be through online forums, social media groups, or local meetups. By fostering a supportive environment, you can help aspiring game designers feel a sense of belonging, find like-minded peers, and gain access to valuable resources and opportunities.

Encourage experimentation and innovation: Emphasize the importance of exploring new ideas, pushing boundaries, and embracing creativity. Encourage aspiring game designers to think outside the box and experiment with unique concepts and mechanics. By fostering an environment that values innovation, you can inspire others to pursue their own unique visions and make a mark in the industry.

Highlight the joy and impact of game design: Showcase the joy and fulfillment that comes from creating games. Share stories of how games have impacted people's lives, whether through entertainment, education, or emotional resonance. By highlighting the positive impact of game design, you can inspire others to channel their passion into a medium that has the potential to touch and connect with people on a deep level.

Ultimately, by sharing your experiences, providing mentorship, showcasing success stories, fostering community, encouraging experimentation, and highlighting the joy of game design, you can inspire and encourage other game designers to pursue their passion and embark on their own rewarding journey in the world of game design.

Closing thoughts on the ever-evolving world of game design

As we reach the end of this book, it's time to reflect on the ever-evolving world of game design and the incredible journey we've embarked on. We've delved into the depths of this fascinating craft, from its humble beginnings to its current position as a thriving industry that captures the hearts of players worldwide.

Being a game designer is more than just a job—it's a passion that ignites our spirits and drives us to create captivating experiences that transport players to extraordinary worlds. The field of game design is alive with constant change and innovation. We must adapt to emerging technologies, evolving player expectations, and shifting industry trends.

The future of game design holds endless excitement and possibilities. Imagine the immersive wonders of virtual reality, the captivating potential of augmented reality, and the transformative impact of artificial intelligence. These advancements will shape the way we play and interact with games, opening new horizons for deeper engagement and storytelling.

As game designers, we wield the power to shape the future of entertainment and leave a lasting impact on players' lives. We must embrace a mindset of curiosity, always seeking new ideas and pushing the boundaries of what is possible. Let us be open to feedback, continuously grow, and nurture a supportive community of fellow designers.

In this ever-changing landscape, collaboration is key. By connecting with our peers, sharing knowledge, and fostering a spirit of camaraderie, we can elevate the art of game design together. Let us celebrate our successes, learn from our challenges, and find inspiration in the joy of play.

As you embark on your own game design journey, hold onto your passion, nurture your creativity, and keep the fun alive. Remember that games are meant to bring joy, wonder, and excitement to players. May your path be filled with thrilling adventures, meaningful connections, and the fulfilment that comes from creating something truly special.

Thank you for joining me on this exploration of the ever-evolving world of game design. May your own journey be a testament to the power of dreams, creativity, and the unwavering pursuit of your passion. Game on, fellow designers!

Appendices

Additional resources for aspiring game designers

Game Design Communities and Forums

- GameDev.net is a vibrant online community where game developers can connect, discuss, and find valuable resources.
- Unity Connect serves as a platform for connecting with other game developers and artists.
- Reddit hosts active communities like r/gamedesign and r/gamedev, offering discussions, feedback, and resources.

Game Design Software and Tools

- Unity, a popular game development engine, provides a comprehensive set of tools and resources.
- Unreal Engine stands out for its graphical capabilities and versatility.
- GameMaker offers a user-friendly approach, making it suitable for beginners.
- If you're interested in narrative-focused games, Twine is an excellent interactive storytelling tool.

Online Courses and Tutorials

- Coursera offers an engaging course called "Introduction to Game Design" by Michigan State University.
- On Udemy, you can check out "Game Design and Development: Create a Game from Scratch" by Ben Tristem and Rick Davidson.
- For insightful videos, head to YouTube channels like Extra Credits, GDC (Game Developers Conference), and Game Maker's Toolkit.

Game Jams and Competitions

- Ludum Dare is a renowned game jam where participants create games based on a given theme

within a limited time frame.
- The Global Game Jam is an annual event where teams from around the world come together to create games over a weekend.
- The Independent Games Festival (IGF) celebrates and honours indie game developers and their creations.

Books
- "The Art of Game Design: A Book of Lenses" by Jesse Schell
- "Game Design Workshop: A Playcentric Approach to Creating Innovative Games" by Tracy Fullerton
- "Challenges for Game Designers" by Brenda Romero and Ian Schreiber
- "Rules of Play: Game Design Fundamentals" by Katie Salen and Eric Zimmerman
- "Game Feel: A Game Designer's Guide to Virtual Sensation" by Steve Swink

Game Design Blogs and Websites
- Gamasutra is a leading source of game development news, articles, and industry insights.
- Game Designing is a valuable blog featuring articles, tutorials, and resources for game designers.
- The Game Design Forum is an online community where you can discuss game design topics and receive feedback.

Networking and Conferences
- The Game Developers Conference (GDC) is an exciting annual event that brings together game developers, industry professionals, and enthusiasts.
- IndieCade is a festival that showcases independent games and offers networking opportunities.
- Don't forget to explore local game development meetups and join game design groups in your area for networking and learning opportunities.

Remember, the world of game design is constantly evolving. These resources will help you enhance your skills, connect with fellow game designers, and fuel your passion for creating unforgettable gaming experiences. Enjoy your journey, and best of luck!

Glossary of basic game design terminology

Aesthetics: The stunning visual and artistic elements of a game, including art style, graphics, colours, and the overall look and feel.

Asset: Any digital or physical element created for a game, such as 3D models, textures, sprites, audio files, or animations.

Balancing: The process of adjusting various game elements, such as difficulty, character abilities, or resource distribution, to ensure a fair and enjoyable experience.

Collaboration: The exciting act of working together with other talented team members, like artists, programmers, sound designers, and producers, to bring the game design to life.

Concept Art: Visual representations, sketches, or illustrations created during the early stages of game design to communicate and explore the artistic direction and style.

Debugging: The process of identifying and fixing software bugs, errors, or glitches in the game's code to enhance its stability and performance.

Game Balance: Ensuring that the gameplay elements, like difficulty, resources, and rewards, are perfectly tuned for a satisfying and fair experience.

Game Design: The exciting process of creating and developing the rules, mechanics, and overall structure of a game.

Game Design Document (GDD): A comprehensive document that outlines the cool concept, gameplay, mechanics, and other design details of a game.

Game Designer: The talented individuals who bring games to life by designing the gameplay mechanics, systems, levels, and overall experience.

Game Development: The magical journey of creating a game from start to finish, involving design, programming, art, audio, and testing.

Game Engine: A software framework or platform that provides the necessary tools, libraries, and functionalities for game development, including rendering, physics, and audio.

Game Feel: The intangible quality that defines the responsiveness, feedback, and overall "feel" of the game's controls, movements, and interactions, contributing to the player's immersion.

Game Loop: The core structure or flow of a game, including the sequence of events, player actions, and feedback that create an engaging and repeatable gameplay experience.

Game World: The virtual or fictional environment in which the game takes place, consisting of locations, landscapes, buildings, and other elements that contribute to the player's immersion.

Iterative Design: The cool approach of continuously refining and improving a game through multiple design iterations based on feedback and testing.

Level Design: The creative art of designing and building the awesome levels or stages within a game, including layout, objectives, and challenges.

Market Research: The process of exploring and analyzing the gaming market, including trends, player preferences, and competitor analysis, to inform design decisions and target the intended audience.

Mechanics: The specific rules, actions, and interactions that govern the gameplay, including character abilities, physics, puzzles, combat systems, or resource management.

Narrative Design: The art of crafting the captivating story, memorable characters, and overall narrative structure of a game.

Player Psychology: The fascinating study of player behavior, motivations, and preferences that helps shape game design decisions for engaging experiences.

Playtesting: The fun process of watching players play and gathering their feedback to improve the game's design, mechanics, and overall experience.

Production: The phase of game development where the game design is turned into reality by implementing the design, creating stunning assets, and assembling the final game.

Prototyping: Creating early versions or mock-ups of a game to playtest and refine its mechanics, systems, and features.

Scope: The overall size, complexity, and features of a game that define its development timeline and the resources needed to make it awesome.

Scope Creep: The phenomenon where the scope of a project gradually expands or exceeds the initial plans, leading to potential delays, increased costs, or reduced quality if not managed effectively.

Simulation: A genre of games that aim to replicate or simulate real-world scenarios, often involving complex systems, physics, or behaviors to provide a realistic or educational experience.

Storyboarding: The process of creating visual representations or sequential sketches to outline the key moments, scenes, or cinematic sequences in a game's narrative or gameplay.

System Mapping: The technique of visually mapping out the interconnected systems, mechanics, and interactions within a game to understand their relationships and ensure cohesive gameplay.

Testing and QA (Quality Assurance): The process of systematically testing the game for bugs, glitches, and issues to ensure a high level of quality and a smooth player experience.

User Experience (UX): The overall experience and satisfaction of players while playing a game, including factors like ease of use, immersion, and enjoyment.

User Interface (UI): The cool visual elements and controls that players use to interact with the game, like menus, buttons, and heads-up display.

User Testing: The practice of observing and gathering feedback from actual players to evaluate and improve the game's usability, mechanics, and overall player experience.

Virtual Reality (VR): An immersive technology that uses headsets or devices to create a simulated 3D environment, enabling players to interact with the game world in a more immersive way.

Visual and Audio Design: The creative process of crafting visually appealing and immersive game worlds, including the game's art style, graphics, and audio elements.

Workflow: The structured and organized sequence of tasks, processes, and activities followed by the game development team to ensure efficient and effective production.

Other Books In The "Video Game" Series by this Author

Please check out some of my other titles on the topic of "Video Games" which is my favourite topic to write about:

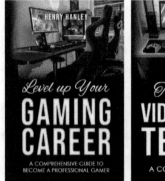  

- **"Level Up Your Gaming Career: A Comprehensive Guide To Become A Professional Gamer"** released in April 2023.

- **"The Art Of Video Games Testing: A Comprehensive Guide"** released in June 2023.

Find these titles on Amazon as an E-book or they can be ordered as a paperback edition where available.

Thank you.

Henry Hanley

www.ingramcontent.com/pod-product-compliance
Lightning Source LLC
LaVergne TN
LVHW051341050326
832903LV00031B/3670